WRITTEN BY TON

52 spurge
STORIES *for* CHILDREN

BOOK 3

A FLY ON THE NOSE
AND 51 OTHER GREAT STORIES

DayOne

Reprinted 2015

British Library Cataloguing in Publication Data available

ISBN 978-1-84625-406-2

Published by Day One Publications
Ryelands Road, Leominster, HR6 8NZ

☎ 01568 613 740
FAX: 01568 611 473
North America Toll Free 888 329 6630
email—sales@dayone.co.uk
web site—www.dayone.co.uk

Cover design by Wayne McMaster

Printed by T J International

To Sally, my wife,
who again has been a great help
in writing this book

CONTENT

Introduction

Charles Haddon Spurgeon was born in 1834, and he died in 1892. After he was converted at the age of fifteen, the Lord used him a great deal. During his long ministry in London, many people came to know the Lord Jesus Christ as their Saviour and Lord. No one else in history up to that time had kept such a large congregation for such a long time.

In the first book, *How a Spider Saved a Man's Life*, I told you about Spurgeon's childhood, how he became a Christian, about his first church in Waterbeach in Cambridgeshire, and then how he became the pastor of what became known as the Metropolitan Tabernacle in London. In the second book, *The Milk's Been Stolen Again*, we had a variety of stories, some concerning amazing conversions, some about the College Spurgeon founded, and others were "all at sea"!

Now, in this third book, the story continues. We think about the Orphanage Spurgeon started; we go to some of the places where he preached; and there are many other interesting stories, too. As before, each has a Bible reference, so that you can learn more about the Lord Jesus Christ and God's will for your life.

1

Something More to Do

"Pure and undefiled religion before
God and the Father is this:
to visit orphans and widows in their trouble ..."
James 1:27

In Britain during the nineteenth century, great numbers of people from the countryside came looking for work in the big cities. Sadly, many were very poor and died quite young, leaving their children as orphans. Sometimes, when fathers died, mothers would find it very difficult to look after their large families. The result was that in London alone, in Spurgeon's time, 100,000 children were not properly cared for. Many didn't have homes as you do, and they would wander the streets, without enough food or clothing. It's hard to imagine how difficult life must have been for them, isn't it?

Spurgeon, of course, saw all this need around him. One day he told his church, the Metropolitan Tabernacle at the Elephant and Castle, "We are a big church, and we should be doing more for the Lord in this great city! Let us ask God to give us something new to do, and if we need money to do it, let's ask the Lord for that, too!"

It so happened that just at that time there was a wealthy Christian widow called Mrs Hillyard. She believed God wanted her to give some of her money away, to help needy children in London! So she asked a friend if he knew of someone reliable and honest who could do this. Her friend immediately said, "Mr Spurgeon!"

Mrs Hillyard had never met Spurgeon, but she wrote to him and said she would give him £20,000 to start an orphanage! Now that was a lot of money. A skilled worker in those days would earn only about £100 a year, so what she wanted to give would be about 3 million pounds in today's money!

Spurgeon decided he would go, with one of his deacons, to see Mrs Hillyard. But her house didn't look very posh—not the kind that a lady who wanted to give away £20,000 would have. So, after meeting her, Spurgeon said, "We have called, Madam, about the £200 you mentioned in your letter." (Is that what she had written?) She said, "£200? Did I write that? I meant to have said £20,000." Spurgeon replied, "Oh yes, you did put £20,000, but I was not sure whether a nought or two had slipped in by mistake, and I thought I would be on the safe side!" Then he said that maybe the money ought to go to her relatives, or be given to George Muller, who ran an orphanage in Bristol. But no, Mrs Hillyard said it was to be for a new children's home in London.

Well, the church had asked the Lord to give them something new to do, and this was it! Within a month, Spurgeon bought some land and soon the Orphanage was built. Later he found out that Mrs Hillyard didn't live in a big, expensive house because she wanted to use her money for doing good to others! Instead of spending it on herself, she wanted to use it for the Lord's work.

Thank God for the comforts of life that you enjoy, and remember also that if you are a believer in the Lord Jesus Christ this will have a practical effect on the way you live. James puts it like this, *"Pure and undefiled religion before God and the Father is this: to visit orphans and widows in their trouble, and to keep oneself unspotted from the world" (James 1:27).*

2
Hope for the Orphans

"Lord, what do You want me to do?"
Acts 9:6

Spurgeon was very pleased that he now had enough money to begin the Orphanage for boys. (Later on, one was opened for girls, too). I'm sure that he was also happy to hear from Mrs Hillyard that she was praying for three things for the boys who entered it. Before you read on, ask yourself: what would you hope for the boys?

The first thing was that every boy should have sufficient food and clothing and be well looked after.

Secondly, she hoped that many of them (if not all!) would become true Christians, believing in the Lord Jesus Christ and following Him all their lives.

Thirdly, her prayer was that many would later become ministers or missionaries.

Well, were your ideas for the boys like Mrs Hillyard's hopes and prayers? I can tell you what happened to the very first boy who came to the Orphanage, whose name was Robert Latimer.

First of all, he was, of course, well looked after during his time there.

Secondly, he did give himself in faith to the Lord Jesus Christ.

But what about her third prayer?

Well, after Robert left the Orphanage he got a job in

London, but soon came to believe that God wanted him to be a pastor. He realized that he needed some training. Wherever could he go for that? Can you guess? If you have read and remembered some of the stories in my second book, you would know straightaway—to the College that Spurgeon began—the Pastors' College! So that is where he went.

After that, Robert pastored four churches, and the Lord blessed and used him very much. Then for seven years he worked for a missionary society called the Russian Evangelization Society.

Mrs Hillyard must have been very pleased that her hopes and prayers for the Orphanage were being answered, even in the very first boy to enter it! Many others also became Christians, and some of them later became pastors and missionaries.

What does God want you to do with your life? He tells you that you should turn from your sin and trust in the Lord Jesus Christ. If you follow Him, you may be sure that He has a plan for you, and there will be things that He wants you to do for Him and ways in which you can serve Him. When Saul (who became the apostle Paul) met the risen Christ on the road to Damascus, he asked the question that you ought to ask, *"Lord, what do You want me to do?" (Acts 9:6).*

3

A Sad Story?

"And we know that all things work together
for good to those who love God,
to those who are the called according to His purpose."
Romans 8:28

Do you remember the third hope and prayer that Mrs Hillyard had for the boys in the Orphanage? It was that some of them might become pastors or missionaries. Now I want to tell you about the first boy who became a missionary, although you might think that this is a very sad story.

His name was John Maynard, and he had come to the Orphanage as a small boy in 1869. He, like all the others, was looked after very well, and he, like many of them, became a Christian. When he was older, he felt that the Lord wanted him to go abroad as a missionary, so he prayed about this, studied and prepared himself. I'm sure he was looking forward very much to going to a foreign country to tell the people there about the Lord Jesus Christ, and how their sins could be forgiven and how they could become children of God. He must have been most excited!

At the age of twenty-five he went to the Congo in Africa. See if you can find the Congo on a map, and then try to work out how many miles he would have to travel to get there from London. Was it 2,000, 4,000, 6,000 or 8,000 miles? (You will find the answer on page 112).

I don't know how long it took him to get there, but it must

have taken quite a while as he had to go by ship. At last he arrived. Now his work could begin!

But he had been there just a few weeks when he died! That seems strange, doesn't it? It seems like a waste! All that praying and training and preparation—and almost as soon as John got to the Congo, he died! He couldn't do much as a missionary in a few weeks, could he?

These were John's last words, "As He will; all is well!"

There are many things that happen in life that we cannot explain—disappointments, illnesses, accidents—all kinds of things. We might wonder why God allows them. We might ask why they have happened to us.

It must have been a disappointment to John when he realized that he was going to die at such a young age, never having been much of a missionary after all. But there is a verse that I'm sure he knew and thought about as he faced his early death: *"And we know that all things work together for good to those who love God, to those who are the called according to His purpose" (Romans 8:28).*

This verse has been a comfort to many Christians when things seem to go wrong in their lives. God will make sure that all things work out for the best for those who love Him, and one day, when we are in heaven, we will know beyond any doubt that God's promise is true. That is why John could say at the end of his young life, "As He will, all is well!"

4

A Large Family in Need

"Every good gift and every perfect gift is from above, and comes down from the Father ..."
James 1:17

There was a great need in London for the Orphanage. In those days, the Government didn't give help and benefits to people as they do today. Many poor families were in desperate situations, and life could be especially hard for children without parents.

In the early days of the Orphanage, Spurgeon himself would see the applicants—usually the widowed mothers. He would listen to their sad stories and often give them some money or other help. The problem was that the Orphanage couldn't accept all the children who were in need, because there were so many of them!

One day a woman came with a great number of children, both boys and girls. Spurgeon spoke to her, and asked her a few questions. She had a very sad story to tell. She had got married, had some children, and then her husband had died. She got married again, had some more children, and then, just recently, her second husband had died. Before marrying her, the second husband had also been married and widowed, and had had some children in that marriage!

What the lady did, which Spurgeon thought rather funny, was this. She separated the children into three groups, and said, "These are his, those are mine, and these are ours!" Can you work that out?

The children of her second husband from his first marriage were "his"; the children of her first marriage were "mine"; and the children of their second marriage were "ours"!

After listening to her, Spurgeon helped her family as much as he could, although I don't know if any of her children came into the Orphanages.

Now, what about you? Do you have enough food to eat? Do you have nice clothes to wear, especially in the winter, when it's cold? And what will you do tonight? Get into a nice, cosy, comfortable bed, and have a refreshing sleep? I expect that you have good food every day, warm clothes, a bed at nighttime, and a home in which to live safe and secure.

Here is something you could do. Get a piece of paper and a pencil or pen, and write down all the good things that you receive each day, the comforts of life, and the people who care for you. There is an old chorus which says:

> Count your blessings, name them one by one,
> Count your blessings, see what God has done,
> Count your blessings, name them one by one,
> And it will surprise you what the Lord has done.

The Bible says, *"Every good gift and every perfect gift is from above, and comes down from the Father ..." (James 1:17)*. We ought to thank Him for all these many good gifts!

5

A Dying Boy

"In My Father's house are many mansions; if it were not so, I would have told you. I go to prepare a place for you."
John 14:2

One Saturday, Spurgeon wanted to show the Orphanage to his friend, John Gough. They rode there in Spurgeon's carriage, and, as usual, the boys were excited to see him! After talking with many of them and giving them all a penny, he said to John, "We have a boy very ill with consumption. He cannot live, and I wish to see him, for he would be disappointed if he knew I had been here and had not seen him."

So they both went into the infirmary at the Orphanage, and there was the boy, lying in bed, very ill. You can imagine how pleased the boy was to see them! Spurgeon sat by his side, held his hand and asked him, "Do you love Jesus?" "Yes," replied the boy.

Spurgeon then said, "Jesus loves you! He bought you with His precious blood, and He knows what is best for you. It seems hard for you to lie here and listen to the shouts of the healthy boys outside at play. But soon Jesus will take you home, and then He will tell you the reason, and you will be so glad!"

Then Spurgeon prayed: "O Jesus, Master, this dear child is reaching out his thin hand to find Yours! Touch him, dear

Saviour, with Your loving, warm clasp. Take him home in Your Own good time. Comfort and cherish him till that good time comes. Show him Yourself as he lies here, and let him see You and know You more and more as his loving Saviour!"

Having finished his prayer he said, "Now, is there anything you would like? Would you like a canary in a cage, to hear him sing?" Seeing that that suggestion appealed to the boy, he turned to the nurse, and said, "Nurse, see that he has a canary tomorrow morning!" Then he spoke again to the boy, "Goodbye! You will see the Saviour, perhaps, before I shall."

John found the whole scene very affecting, and later he said, regarding his friend Spurgeon, "I have seen him hold, by his power, six thousand five hundred people. I know him as a great man, but as he sat by the bedside of a dying pauper child, whom he had rescued, he was to me a greater and grander man than when swaying the mighty multitude in his preaching!"

That ill boy hadn't much longer to live, but Spurgeon was able to comfort him with the knowledge that when he died he would go to be with the Lord Jesus. Spurgeon was able to give him a canary, but Jesus gave him and promised him much more! Those who love Him go to be with Him when they die. Here is His promise to them: *"In My Father's house are many mansions; if it were not so, I would have told you. I go to prepare a place for you" (John 14:2).*

6

A Little Boy Called Bob

"Give us this day our daily bread."
Matthew 6:11

Spurgeon was so concerned and interested in the Orphanage children that he would often visit them, and they would be very pleased to see him. They looked upon him, I suppose, a little like their grandfather! He knew nearly all of them by name.

One day, he was sitting on a seat in the grounds talking with a friend, while the children were playing all round, when a little boy, about eight years old, came up and said, "Please, Mr Spurgeon, I want to come and sit down on that seat between you two gentlemen!" "Come along then, Bob," said Spurgeon, "and tell us what you want."

"Please, Mr Spurgeon," said Bob, "suppose there was a little boy who had no father, who lived in an Orphanage with a lot of other little boys who had no father; and suppose those little boys had mothers and aunts who comed once a month, and brought them apples and oranges, and gave them pennies; and suppose this little boy had no mother, and no aunt, and so nobody never came to bring him nice things—don't you think somebody ought to give him a penny?"

Can you guess who Bob was referring to?

He continued, "'Cause, Mr Spurgeon, that's me!"

(As you can tell, Bob's English wasn't very good, was it? Can you put it right?)

Spurgeon considered what Bob had said. It did sound reasonable, didn't it? If other boys had presents from their families, and poor little Bob had no visitors or gifts, it was very unfair! Now Spurgeon was always very kind, especially to people in need, and Bob knew that! So it was that he gave Bob six pennies, and he went away happy! In fact Spurgeon made sure that he and others like him in the Orphanage got pocket money regularly.

Why do you think that Bob went to Spurgeon like that?

First, he must have felt that Spurgeon, although talking to a friend, wouldn't mind being interrupted. Secondly, he believed that Spurgeon would listen to him. Thirdly, he knew that Spurgeon was kind-hearted and likely to sympathize with him and his situation. And in the fourth place, he believed that Spurgeon could give him what he wanted.

Now, instead of thinking about Bob and Spurgeon, think about yourself and the Lord. He is never too busy, so you cannot interrupt Him! He is always ready and willing to listen to His children. He is kind and sympathetic. And He can give you what you need. For example, Jesus taught His disciples to pray, *"Give us this day our daily bread" (Matthew 6:11)*. In all our need, if we are truly trusting Him, we can go to Him, and He will be pleased to listen and answer us!

7

A Frightening Storm!

"And this is eternal life, that they may know You, the only true God, and Jesus Christ ..."
John 17:3

I'm sure that sometimes you have been outside when it has started to rain really hard. On one occasion that happened to Spurgeon when he and a friend were walking together in the grounds of the Orphanage. It was a real downpour so they took shelter in the gymnasium there. Many of the boys were already there, and when they saw Spurgeon coming in, they gave a tremendous cheer!

Outside the weather was getting worse and worse, and a storm developed, with thunder and lightning. Someone brought Spurgeon a chair, and he sat down with the boys around him. The storm increased, and became quite frightening, with flash after flash of lightning!

Then Spurgeon told the boys about a young Christian who some years before was in his uncle's house one night, during a terrible storm. (In fact he was talking about himself!) A baby was upstairs, but nobody felt brave enough to go up to get the baby down because they didn't want to go past a big window on the stairs in case the lightning flashed just then! But Spurgeon decided that he would go up and bring the baby down because he trusted in the Lord! So that is what he did.

While Spurgeon was speaking, the storm increased, and the sky got darker and darker. One of the boys suggested singing a hymn which you might know: "Abide with me, fast falls the eventide; the darkness deepens, Lord, with me abide." When they finished singing, Spurgeon spoke about how sins are forgiven, and how to have the peace of God. As he did so, the flashes of lightning and the peals of thunder continued! Then they sang another well-known hymn, "Like a river glorious is God's perfect peace." He then spoke about the cross on which Jesus died, although by now the noise of the rain on the roof as well as the thunder made it very difficult to hear all he said! So they sang again. This time it was: "How sweet the Name of Jesus sounds in a believer's ear; it soothes his sorrows, heals his wounds, and drives away his fear."

Then they heard what sounded like a loud rifle crack, and they thought that something very close by had been struck by lightning! The boys looked fearfully at one another! This time Spurgeon told them that all the people who ran the Orphanages had this one great desire—that each boy and girl there might trust in the Lord Jesus Christ as their own Saviour. A little later they all sang the great doxology, "Praise God, from Whom all blessings flow ..."

As they sang that, the storm stopped, and someone said to Spurgeon, "The boys will never forget this! It will abide with them throughout eternity!"

You may like to look up those hymns and see if you can find out who wrote them. Here's a clue: the authors are Frances Havergal, Thomas Ken, Henry Lyte and John Newton—but who wrote which hymn? It's good to know the hymns, but it's better to know the Saviour. He said, *"And this is eternal life, that they may know You, the only true God, and Jesus Christ Whom You have sent" (John 17:3).*

8

Sad News from the Orphanage

"Therefore you also be ready, for the
Son of Man is coming at an hour
when you do not expect."
Matthew 24:44

Some other time I'll tell you some stories of the visits that Spurgeon made to Europe. He would often stay in a town in southern France called Menton—see if you can find it on a map.

Sometimes people away from home receive sad news, and that is what happened to Spurgeon one day when he was in Menton. Maybe you can guess what the news was, now that you have read the first seven stories about the Orphanage. Yes, the sad news was that one of the boys there had died. What could he do? He couldn't return home just then, so he decided to send a letter to all the boys there.

This is what he wrote: "I wonder who will be next! Dear boys, would you go to heaven if you were now at once to die? Wait a bit, and let each one answer for himself. You know, you must be born again, you must repent of sin, you must believe in Jesus. How is it with you? If you are not saved, you are in great danger, in fearful peril! Be warned, I pray you! I cannot bear to think of one boy going from the Orphanage to hell; that would be terrible indeed!

"I often think about you all. I want to see you all happy here and hereafter. May you grow up to be honourable Christian men; and if God should take any of you away, may we all meet in heaven. Will you pray a special prayer, just now, that the death of one boy may bring all of you to Jesus to find eternal life?"

I expect that the boys in the Orphanage were very sorry when the boy died—they probably knew him well. When they received Spurgeon's letter it must have made them think about themselves and their own relationship with God. I wonder if any of them trusted in the Lord Jesus as a result of that letter.

You may have heard someone refer to the Lord either 'coming or calling'. Do you know what that means? One day we will leave time and go into eternity, and it will be either in our lifetime when the Lord Jesus comes again to bring about the end of the world, or when we are called into His presence by death. Nobody knows when He will come or when He will call. That is why He said, *"Therefore you also be ready, for the Son of Man is coming at an hour when you do not expect" (Matthew 24:44).*

9

What About the Old?

"Honor widows who are really widows."
1 Timothy 5:3

Well, we've thought about the children at the Orphanage, but what about elderly people? We ought to respect and honour those who are older. Was the Metropolitan Tabernacle concerned about them?

Spurgeon started the Orphanage and the College, but he didn't have to start a work for older people because when he went to be the pastor there was already an Old Ladies' Home! This had been founded about fifty years before he arrived, and I'll tell you how it began.

The pastor in those days was a man called John Rippon. He saw the need all around him: there were many older ladies and widows who hadn't much money, and life was very hard for them. He spoke to the deacons of the church about it, but they said, "The expense will be enormous! We can't afford it! We could never get enough money!"

Well, John went on about it, and the deacons kept saying, "No!"

In the end he said, "I'll go out next Monday and try and collect five hundred pounds before the evening meeting." (That was a lot of money then.) "If I get the money we'll go ahead, and if I don't we'll drop the idea." The deacons thought, "He'll never get five hundred pounds in one day!" So they agreed.

Monday evening came, and the deacons met, expecting to hear John say that he had tried, but just couldn't collect all that money. Imagine their surprise when he said, "There is eight hundred pounds which I got almost without asking, and there is more promised!" So then the deacons thought starting a home for older ladies was a good idea, and they wanted to be in on this new venture. But John said, "No, no! I shall not need your services! You have opposed me all along, and now I have done the work without you! You can attend to something else!"

A Trust Deed is a legal document setting out the rules concerning an organization, and John made sure that the Trust Deed for the Old Ladies' Home stated that the pastor would choose the ladies who could live there, with "no deacon interfering"!

Spurgeon greatly supported this Home. When the Metropolitan Tabernacle was built the Home itself was moved to be very near the church, so that the elderly ladies could easily get there. Not only did they have a home in which to live but they were given food and clothing and other necessities. Spurgeon was so interested and generous that sometimes bills were paid twice, because he personally and quietly paid them, and then the church paid them as well!

God says that we should give respect to those who are older, and, if they are in need, do what we can to help them. Paul tells Timothy that the local church should especially do this for older ladies in the fellowship: *"Honor those who are really widows" (1 Timothy 5:3).*

10

No Entry!

"Strive to enter through the narrow gate,
for many, I say to you, will seek to
enter and will not be able."
Luke 13:24

Now I want to tell you about some of the places Spurgeon visited to preach the Word of God. His church, of course, was in London, but he was invited to speak in many different parts of Britain.

On one occasion he was asked to speak in Glasgow. (In which country is that? See if you can find it on a map.) He went along there with the Lord Provost of Glasgow, a very important person in the city. They got to the City Hall, and at the door was a policeman checking that everybody entering had a ticket. Well, neither Spurgeon nor the Provost had been given a ticket.

The policeman said, "I can't let you in, for you haven't got a ticket!" The Provost said, "But you must let us in!" The policeman replied, "I cannot, no matter who you are!"

Spurgeon said, "This is the Lord Provost!"

But the policeman was unmoved. "I don't know about that, nor do I care who he is! I have my orders from the inspector to let nobody in without a ticket, and I am sure the Lord Provost wouldn't wish me to disobey orders."

The Provost then said, "But this is Mr Spurgeon! And he has to deliver the lecture!"

Still the policeman wouldn't change his mind. "I cannot help that. I have my orders, and he shall not come in without a ticket!"

Spurgeon and the Provost went on and on talking and reasoning and arguing, but it was no good! The policeman did his duty, obeyed his orders, and wouldn't let them in! Lots of people were going into the Hall to hear Spurgeon speak, but he couldn't even get into the building! Well, what was to be done? In the end the two men had a good idea. They both had cards with their names on, and they persuaded the policeman to send these cards in to the inspector, and as soon as the inspector saw them, he gave orders to the policeman to allow Spurgeon and the Provost to enter.

Spurgeon later drew out a lesson from this amusing but frustrating experience. Our sins will keep us out of God's kingdom. Our sins say, "You cannot come in! Go away! No entry for you!" But we must be really determined to get in. We should be saying, "I must have my sins forgiven! I must know Jesus Christ as my Saviour and Lord! I must come in!" It was along these lines that Jesus said, *"Strive to enter through the narrow gate, for many, I say to you, will seek to enter and will not be able" (Luke 13:24).*

11

Another Terrible Storm!

"Therefore you also be ready."
Luke 12:40

If it's pouring down with rain, we all try and find a place to shelter, but if there is thundering and lightning, do you know where you should not go? Under a tree! It's better to get very wet than to stand under a tree in a thunderstorm!

Well, a man was walking on Clapham Common in South London when a terrible storm came. The rain came down, the thunder boomed and the lightning flashed! Unwisely, the man took shelter under a tree, the tree was struck by lightning, and the man was killed.

Spurgeon heard about the tragedy, and decided to go and preach right there, and for two reasons. The first you can probably guess—he wanted to tell people about the Lord Jesus Christ, because no one knows when he or she is going to die, and we all need to be saved and forgiven by Him so that we are ready when death comes to us.

But what about the other reason? Here's a clue—think of the man's widow. Spurgeon thought it would be a very good idea to have a collection under the tree for her, so that she would have enough money to live on now that her husband had died. Maybe she also had children to look after.

The meeting was arranged, and a wagon acted as a pulpit. Spurgeon's text was, *"Therefore you also be ready" (Luke 12:40)*. He said that, thankfully, very few people are killed by lightning. We needn't be afraid of storms, but in a bad one, avoid trees! "When such a solemn event occurs, we ought to hear in it the voice of God, and listen to what He says to us."

He then referred to the fact that in St. Paul's Cathedral (which is a famous church in London) there is a little chisel mark. A man had been working on the dome, when suddenly he fell, and was killed. I've never heard about that, but next time I go there I must try to find it!

He said, "What a solemn spot is that; and what a solemn spot is this. My dear hearers, before you go away, pray for pardon; and, as often as you pass this place, think of your past lives, and of the world to come. But, my dear friends, before you go away this afternoon, will not each one of you pray for himself that his sins may be pardoned? Lift up your hearts to God, and every one of you cry, 'God be merciful to me a sinner!' Look this very instant to Christ Jesus, Who died upon the cross!"

I'm sure the widow in her sorrow was nevertheless grateful for the collection that was made, and it must have been a great help to her. And I expect the people there realized what a solemn occasion that was, standing around a tree which had been struck by lightning where a man suddenly lost his life. The Lord Jesus said we should all be ready!

12

How Many in Church?

"Whatever your hand finds to do, do it with your might."
Ecclesiastes 9:10

Usually thousands of people would go to hear Spurgeon, whether it was in his own church or anywhere else. On one occasion some Christians in a place called Isleham in Cambridgeshire invited him to preach. You could look this town up on a map.

Spurgeon agreed to go; there were to be services in the morning and the evening. There was also to be one in the afternoon at which someone else would preach. The people who arranged the meetings thought, "Spurgeon is a very popular preacher, and lots and lots of people will want to hear him, so we'd better hire the biggest church building in the town!" And that is what they did.

So the day came, and Spurgeon went up into the pulpit to begin the first service at eleven o'clock. He looked round at his congregation. Can you guess how many were there? Not seven thousand, not seven hundred, not seventy—but only seven! I'm sure that was a surprise for everyone, and not a happy one either! He said, "You borrowed this big place for seven people?"

What did Spurgeon do? Of course, he preached as well as he could, looking to the Lord to help him. It's good if many people go to hear the preaching of God's Word, but even if only a very few are there, the Lord ought to be praised and His Word proclaimed.

Later the man who was to preach in the afternoon said to Spurgeon, "I can't think how you did it! You were as earnest and preached as well as if you had had the place full!"

In the afternoon the congregation was larger—there were between a hundred and a hundred and fifty present. But what about the evening meeting? How many were there? Seven? A hundred? A hundred and fifty? I don't know! But I can tell you this—the place was so packed that there was not even standing room for any more! All the seats were filled, and every other space in the building. There wasn't room for one more!

What had happened was this: because Spurgeon preached so well in the morning to the seven, they went away and told others and encouraged them to come, and so in the evening the place was full!

I wonder if Spurgeon was disappointed at the small morning congregation and felt it hadn't been worth coming all that way from London to Isleham just to speak to seven people. He could have been preaching to many more in his own church! Maybe he felt discouraged! But I'm sure he knew this verse: *"Whatever your hand finds to do, do it with your might" (Ecclesiastes 9:10).*

Perhaps you haven't got very important things to do in your life, and you feel that it's hardly worth doing them, and are tempted to give up! But remember, it is the Lord Who has given you these things to do. If you do them for Him to the best of your ability that will please Him.

13

Help!

"God be merciful to us and bless us, and cause His face to shine upon us ..."
Psalm 67:1

We're off again on our travels with Spurgeon, and this time we're going to Bristol. I hope that you are following all his journeys on a map!

It was a Wednesday, and he went there to speak at the opening of a new church. There were to be two meetings—one in the afternoon and another in the evening. The afternoon one was due to start at 2.30 p.m., but an hour before that, great crowds came, and as soon as the doors were opened they rushed in and every seat was taken!

That wasn't too bad, but in the evening even more people came. The building was crowded, the passages were packed, and there were thousands of people outside. Some were so eager to hear Spurgeon and so frustrated at not being able to enter that they started knocking on the walls trying to get in! No one seemed able to control them. Crowds of people inside and crowds of people outside! The meeting started, but there was so much noise that Spurgeon said, "I have too many people to hear me! I wish that some other preacher would preach to half of the people here, and I could preach to the other half."

I expect he was thinking of the danger posed by so many people not only in the church building, but those outside.

Maybe some might get hurt in the crush, and even possibly fights might break out. So he went on to say, "I hope that someone will go to the police station for help!" Well, that was a good idea, but how could anyone in the building force his way through the crowd to get outside in order to reach the police station? Someone found a solution. One man volunteered to be let down out of one of the windows by a rope, and in that way he eventually got help from the police to control the crowds!

Spurgeon said, "I wish I had the strength I had a few years ago! I have preached ten times a week! I am getting old before I am young!" How old do you think he was? He sounds like an old man, doesn't he? In fact he was only twenty-seven! He was giving himself so completely and selflessly to the Lord's work, that he was wearing himself out. Of course, he did preach in that church at the evening meeting, but only for a short while because he was feeling very tired and exhausted.

I sometimes wonder how many would come and listen to Spurgeon if he were alive now. We just don't know, do we? Crowds today go to football matches and to watch other sports, and they go to concerts of one kind or another in great numbers—but they don't often go to hear the preaching of God's Word. We should pray that the Lord would give people an interest in hearing the gospel. The Psalmist prayed for this in *Psalm 67:1–2: "God be merciful to us and bless us, And cause His face to shine upon us. That Your way may be known on earth, Your salvation among all nations."*

14

A Practical Sermon

"He who despises his neighbor sins;
but he who has mercy on the poor, happy is he."
Proverbs 14:21

Get your map out again! This time we're off to a town called Tring, in Hertfordshire. I don't think that Spurgeon had gone there to preach, but once the people of the town knew that he was there, they wanted to hear him. But, of course, they had made no arrangements, and so the big question was—where could the meeting be held?

They asked the pastor of the local church, but he said, "No!" He didn't want Spurgeon preaching in his church! Then they asked the vicar of the parish church, but he also said, "No!"

The people then thought of holding the meeting in the open air, but it was winter and very cold, so that was no good! Where could they meet? Spurgeon had to leave the town early the next morning, so it was that day or not at all! Sadly, it looked as if they wouldn't be able to hear him after all.

However, a farmer heard about it, and offered the use of a large barn. A pulpit of sorts was quickly built, and long before the meeting was due to start the place was crowded!

Spurgeon arrived, and told the congregation that he had been asked to give only one sermon, but that he would give two! Well, he gave the first one—I don't know what the text was, but I'm sure he preached about the gospel and the Lord Jesus Christ. The people listened very well.

But what about his second sermon? It was much shorter than the first one. Can you guess what it was about? Here's a clue—the farmer was very poor. Spurgeon paused, then he said, "And now for sermon number two—a plain, practical sermon! Our friend [and he meant the farmer] who gave us the use of this building, is a poor man. When I saw him this morning he wore a coat all in tatters; his shirt absolutely grinned at me through the holes! Let us show our appreciation for his kindness by buying him a new suit of clothes!"

In a few minutes, ten or twelve pounds had been collected, which in those days was enough to buy some good clothes. When Spurgeon got back to his church in London, he told the people there about what had happened, and some of them had a collection, too, and were able to send an extra twenty pounds to the farmer!

As Spurgeon said, his second sermon especially was a very practical one. The Bible says, *"He who despises his neighbor sins; but he who has mercy on the poor, happy is he" (Proverbs 14:21)*. But when you come to think of it, all sermons ought to have a practical result and should affect the way we live. When you next hear a sermon, or read the Bible, ask yourself, "How can I put this into practice? What does this mean I should do?"

15

Persistence!

"Men always ought to pray and not lose heart."
Luke 18:1

In a village somewhere in England there was a small Baptist church, too small and too poor to have a pastor. Among the members, there was a godly old gardener who made arrangements for the visiting preachers, and also an elderly couple who put those preachers up from Saturday until Monday each weekend. Their cottage was small, and their food plain, but the warmth of their hearts and their generous welcome more than made up for that.

The old gardener got it into his head that he would like Spurgeon to preach at his church, so he wrote and asked him to come. Spurgeon wrote back and said that he was sorry, but he couldn't manage it. That didn't put the old man off! He wrote again, and again got the same reply. Then he wrote a third time, and the answer was as before. But he was determined, so he wrote a fourth time, saying that he would continue to write until Spurgeon came! I think that Spurgeon was getting a bit fed up by then, and of course he had many other letters to answer, and many other invitations from all over the place to preach, so he didn't reply to this fourth letter. But was that gardener persistent! He would regularly send a letter, until he had written dozens of them!

Spurgeon, in the meantime, had heard that the old gardener was a godly man, and so in the end he agreed to preach in the church one weekday. He also heard of the elderly couple's kindness and hospitality, and said that when he came he would like to have a meal with them.

As the day approached, notices were put up in the villages around. The local squire found out and, knowing that Spurgeon was very famous, immediately wrote to him offering him hospitality at his big house. Spurgeon wrote back, thanking the squire for his kindness, but telling him about this godly old couple who had for years looked after the preachers every week, and that he was to stay with them. But he did have a suggestion—that the squire send supplies of food to the couple, and that he also join them for dinner and tea! And the squire agreed.

The day came. The old couple got their little cottage nice and clean. Spurgeon was there, and the squire, and the gardener, and there sat the couple in their Sunday best—with all this food, and with the squire's servants waiting on them in their humble home!

One of Spurgeon's friends went to preach in that church a couple of years' later, and had hospitality with the same old couple. The wife went to a corner cupboard, unlocked it, and took a cup and saucer from the shelf. She said, "There, that is the very cup and saucer out of which Mr Spurgeon had his tea! It has never been used since. But in honour of your visit to us, I am going to give you your tea in it! But do be sure you don't break it!"

How was it that the gardener got Spurgeon to preach in his church? He had persistence! He went on and on until he got what he wanted! Jesus spoke about that in the parable of the persistent widow, which begins in this way, *"Then He spoke a parable to them to this end, that men always ought to pray and not lose heart" (Luke 18:1)*. You can read the parable in the first eight verses of that chapter—the widow, like the gardener, persisted and persevered until she got what she wanted.

16

Forms

"But what things were gain to me, these
I have counted loss for Christ."
Philippians 3:7

On another occasion Spurgeon was going to preach somewhere, and, as usual, lots of people wanted to hear him. The organizers had to get as many seats as they could, and they also managed to get some forms as well. Do you know what a form is? The word has a few meanings, which are important for this story. But a form can mean a bench—that is, a long seat without a back.

So the day came, Spurgeon arrived, and the meeting started. All the people were listening to him, when something unexpected and startling happened. Suddenly one of the forms broke, and all those sitting on it found themselves in awkward and silly-looking positions—some on the ground, others leaning over at strange angles!

Spurgeon stopped speaking and asked, "Where did you get those forms?" When someone told him, he replied, "Oh, then you did not borrow them from the Church of England? Well then, you see our forms cannot be trusted any more than theirs!"

You may like to look up the word 'form' in a dictionary. I looked it up in mine, and there are lots of meanings! Here are some of them. Can you work out which one Spurgeon was meaning?

- shape
- system
- ceremony
- behaviour
- school class
- the bed of a hare
- criminal record

Spurgeon was referring to ceremonies. In the Church of England and in many other churches there are set ceremonies, and certain words have to be repeated at each service by the minister. But we cannot trust those ceremonies or words to save us. Going through rituals or using special set words, forms of that kind, cannot get you to heaven! Maybe your church doesn't have those things in its services. Instead, it could be that believers are baptized, and they also regularly attend the Lord's Supper where they eat bread to remember that Jesus' body was broken, and they drink from a cup to remember that His blood was spilt for them. Those things are forms as well. But they cannot save you, either. That was what Spurgeon was getting at. It is only trust in the Lord Jesus Christ that can save you and get you safely to heaven.

The apostle Paul was Jewish, and as he grew up he went through all the Jewish rituals and forms, and in his earlier years he trusted those things to try to make himself right with God. He writes about it in his letter to the Philippians, chapter three. Then he was converted on the road to Damascus. He had met the risen Lord Jesus, and he trusted in Him alone! That saved him—not all those other forms. He wrote, *"But what things were gain to me, these I have counted loss for Christ" (Philippians 3:7).*

What outward forms cannot do for us, Jesus can do!

17

Near-Misses

"My times are in Your hand."
Psalm 31:15

Accidents are happening all the time. Some people, instead of trusting God, believe in luck and chance. If they escape from some disaster, they say, "I was lucky!" Spurgeon, on a number of occasions, was saved from serious accidents and disasters, and he knew that it was not because of luck, but because the Lord was looking after him. Let me tell you of some of his escapes.

On one occasion, he stayed in an inn on the Isle of Wight. (You'd better get the map out again!) It had a thatched roof. (Are there any thatched cottages near where you live?) He stayed until the Saturday, but needed to get back to London to preach in the Tabernacle the next day. But on that Sunday, when Spurgeon was safely back in his own church, there was a terrible storm on the Isle of Wight, and a tall elm tree was blown down and destroyed the very room in which he had stayed!

Another time, he was in Scotland in a horse-drawn carriage. Part of the harness broke, and the horse and carriage—with Spurgeon in it—went rushing down a hill, out of control. There was nothing he or anyone else could do to stop the horse or direct it. When it reached the bottom of the hill it had to turn either left or right. If it turned left, at such great speed, the carriage, taking the corner, would have toppled over, but if it turned right, there was a mound or bank that would stop the carriage from being turned over. Which way would the horse go? Well, it turned right, the carriage didn't crash, and soon horse and carriage came to a standstill—and Spurgeon was safe!

On one of his annual visits to the south of France, he travelled by a different train from his usual one. Later he learnt that the train he normally caught was involved in an accident, and many people had been injured.

Spurgeon was speaking in Halifax. A huge wooden structure was erected specially for the occasion, so that many people could hear him preach God's Word. Six thousand people came. Two meetings were held, and it was a snowy day. Now snow is very heavy. Maybe you have rolled snow along the ground, so that the ball of snow gets bigger and bigger—and heavier and heavier! After the evening meeting, as the people were leaving, one of the supports holding up the gallery gave way because of the weight of the snow on the canvas roof, and two people got their legs broken. Three hours after all the people had left, the whole building collapsed. Spurgeon said that if that had happened during the meeting many people would have been killed, and that may have included him!

Those were 'near-misses', weren't they? If Spurgeon had stayed another night in that inn on the Isle of Wight, if the horse had turned to the left instead of the right, if he had caught his usual train in France, or if the roof had collapsed a few hours earlier, perhaps Spurgeon would have been seriously hurt or even killed. Was it luck or chance? No! God is in control of all things, and His will is done. That doesn't mean that we will never have an accident, but it does mean that if we trust Him, we never need be afraid. The Psalmist said, *"My times are in Your hand" (Psalm 31:15).*

18

When and Where Can You Pray?

"Pray without ceasing."
1 Thessalonians 5:17

Can you answer this question: 'What is prayer?'

Maybe you have seen a very helpful little book called 'A Catechism for Boys and Girls'. A catechism is a book of questions and answers based on the teachings of the Bible. The answer in that particular catechism to the question about prayer is this: 'Prayer is talking with God.'

It is a wonder that ordinary, sinful people can talk to God. He is completely holy, which means that He can have nothing to do with sin or evil. Our sins would keep us away from God, so that we could never talk to Him. But He sent His Son, the Lord Jesus Christ, to save His people from their sins, and so if we trust in Jesus and His death upon the cross we can have fellowship with God as our Father, we can talk to Him in prayer and listen to Him talking to us through His Word, the Bible.

You cannot just go and talk to the Queen or the Prime Minister, but if you trust in Jesus you can go right into God's presence and talk to Him, and know that He listens to you.

But when and where can we pray? Jesus, in His Sermon on the Mount, said, "But when you pray, go into your room, and when you have shut your door, pray to your Father Who is in the secret place" (Matthew 6:6). All Christians should have a regular, daily quiet time alone with the Lord, speaking and listening to Him. You know also that when God's people meet in church, they pray. There are many examples of this in the New Testament. But you don't have to be in your room and you don't have to be in church to pray. You can pray anywhere and everywhere!

Spurgeon, of course, prayed. But he wasn't the kind of person who would wake up every morning at four o'clock and spend six hours in prayer! John Knox, who was a great Reformer in Scotland, had a son-in-law called John Welch, who would spend three-quarters of every day in prayer! I don't know how he managed that! Not many people could do that. Spurgeon said, "I do not feel the call or necessity for such an arrangement. I generally spend but a few minutes, sometimes only moments in prayer at a time. I take a promise, and plead it, or I lay my case before God, and leave it. I do not see that more is required."

But Spurgeon was always conscious of the Lord and ready to pray. One day he was on a railway journey with some friends. He had a great sense of humour, and so it was for them all a very happy time. Suddenly he said, "Brethren, I have just remembered something! Let us pray about it together!" He told them what he had just remembered, and then led them in prayer.

There is a very short verse in the apostle Paul's first letter to the Thessalonians: *"Pray without ceasing" (1 Thessalonians 5:17).*

19

Whose Sermon?

"I will hear what God the LORD will speak,
for He will speak peace to His people and to His saints ..."
Psalm 85:8

Sometimes Christians get sad and depressed and wonder if they are God's children at all—doubts come into their minds and they feel more and more miserable. One Sunday, Spurgeon was feeling like this. He wasn't preaching that day, which was unusual, and maybe a good thing, too! He wasn't in London either, but in a country town somewhere in England.

Some believers, when they are feeling very low, stay away from church, which is precisely the wrong thing to do! Spurgeon was wise enough to know that, whether he felt like it or not, whether he was happy or sad, he ought to go and worship the Lord on Sundays, and so he went to the local church. The preacher that day wasn't a pastor—in fact he normally worked as an engineer—but occasionally he would speak on Sundays. He was what we sometimes call a 'lay preacher'.

Spurgeon listened to the Bible reading as we should all do, and then to the sermon. He was eager to hear what the Lord's message to him would be. For him, it turned out to be a wonderful message, and God spoke to him very clearly through it. As he listened, his depression left him, and he was convinced, once again, that he was a true believer and that he was really trusting in the Lord Jesus Christ. His doubts all vanished, and he rejoiced again in the fact that he was a child of God.

He knew that the Lord's servants need encouragement sometimes, especially if He uses them to bless others, so after the service he went to the preacher and said, "I thank you very much for that sermon!" The preacher hadn't recognized Spurgeon, so he asked, "Who are you?" "Spurgeon!" came the answer.

Then the preacher went as red as a beetroot because he was so embarrassed! And do you know why?

He said, "Why, it was one of your sermons that I preached this morning!" He had got hold of a copy of one of Spurgeon's sermons and preached that instead of preparing his own!

Spurgeon replied, "Yes, I know it was; but that was the very message that I wanted to hear!"

Spurgeon had one of his own sermons preached to him, and God had spoken to him through it!

God speaks to us today through His Word, the Bible, and good sermons and books can help us to understand its meaning. When we go to church and listen to a sermon, we should say, *"I will hear what God the LORD will speak, for He will speak peace to His people and to His saints, but let them not turn back to folly" (Psalm 85:8).*

20
Heaven

"And God will wipe away every tear from their eyes;
there shall be no more death, nor sorrow, nor crying;
and there shall be no more pain ..."
Revelation 21:4

One day Spurgeon was speaking in an English village chapel, and he was preaching about heaven. He mentioned the glories of heaven, how wonderful a place it is, and how amazing it will be to be there. I don't know what his Bible passage was, or exactly what he said, but there are many references to heaven in God's Word. Maybe this was his text: *"And God will wipe away every tear from their eyes; there shall be no more death, nor sorrow, nor crying; and there shall be no more pain, for the former things have passed away" (Revelation 21:4).*

Heaven certainly sounds a wonderful place, doesn't it? It is a place where nobody ever dies, so there will be no funerals and no cemeteries. Can you imagine never feeling sad or sorrowful? In this world many things happen which make us sad, but in heaven nobody ever feels like that. Have you ever cried? I'm sure you have, but up there you will never see a tear in anyone's eye. And what about pain? We all know what it is to suffer. Nobody in heaven ever needs to take any medicine, or go to the doctor, or stay in hospital. No accidents or illnesses, no medicines, no doctors, no hospitals! Heaven is a glorious place, and best of all is the fact that the Saviour, the

Lord Jesus Christ, is there. He is at the centre of heaven! He makes heaven heaven!

Next time you are in church listening to a sermon, remember that preachers look round, and see each person in the congregation, and they notice if people are looking interested or if they seem to be thinking of other things. Well, that day Spurgeon looked round, and especially noticed a lady with a very nice, big smile on her face! She listened to him talk about heaven, and as she thought about it she was filled with joy! She was looking forward to going there.

Later, he looked at her again, and saw that she still had that smile on her face. But then he noticed that she wasn't moving at all! She smiled, and then had completely stopped moving! Why? What had happened? Can you guess?

Spurgeon said, "Friends, I think that our sister over there is dead!" At once, some of the people went over to her, and he was quite right—she had died! They carried her body out of church, and her death in the middle of the sermon made a big impression on everyone there, especially upon Spurgeon himself. I'm sure that nobody who was there that day ever forgot what had happened, or the subject of the sermon they heard—heaven!

When you come to think of it, wasn't that a wonderful way for a Christian to die—hearing about the glories of heaven, and, while hearing, to go straight there? I've heard people say, "Be good, or you won't go to heaven!" The trouble is, none of us can ever be good enough to go there. That is why we need the Saviour. Only by trusting in Him can we get to that beautiful place. I hope that you will go there, and find out for yourself how wonderful and glorious heaven is.

21

Stars

"When I consider Your heavens, the work of Your fingers, the moon and the stars, which You have ordained ..."
Psalm 8:3

Spurgeon liked visiting Scotland, with its wonderful mountains and glens. Maybe you have been there, or maybe you even have the pleasure of living there, like I do! One day he was in a beautiful Scottish glen with one of his friends, who was also the pastor of a church—a Mr Williams. They were chatting about various things, when Spurgeon had an idea.

He said, "Give me a text, Williams, and I will preach you a sermon!"

If someone said that to you, which text from the Bible would you choose? Maybe you would pick a well-known verse, like John's Gospel, chapter three and verse sixteen. Do you know what that says? It's a very good verse to memorize. Look it up and do your best to remember it word for word.

But Williams didn't choose that verse, in fact he didn't choose any very familiar text. He knew Spurgeon well, and he didn't want to make it easy for him. He tried to think of a verse that he hoped would be difficult to preach from. He viewed it as a challenge! He thought about it, and at last this was the verse he chose, and especially the end part: "There is one glory of the sun, another glory of the moon, and another glory of the stars; for one star differs from another star in glory" (1 Corinthians 15:41). I don't think many preachers would want to preach from that verse, at least not on the spur of the moment—I know I wouldn't!

Now Spurgeon was really a very clever man, and he knew a great deal about many things. At once he began his impromptu sermon by describing the glory of certain special stars of separate constellations, giving in each case the name and their position in the heavens, until Williams listened in wonder, and wished that he could write it all down! He said, looking back on that amazing sermon, "Never have I heard him do anything more sublime, even when preaching to gathered thousands!"

Spurgeon must have often looked up at the stars, and he had learnt a lot about them. Someone mentioned in the Bible also looked at the sky—King David. He wrote, "*When I consider Your heavens, the work of Your fingers, the moon and the stars, which You have ordained, what is man that You are mindful of him, and the son of man that You visit him?" (Psalm 8:3–4).*

If it's nighttime now (or, if it's daytime, later on when it's dark), look out of your window and see if you can see any stars. How far away they are, up there, twinkling in the night sky! And then think, as David did, that God made them all—and many more that we can't see. He is the God Who created all things. Then think of the wonderful fact that this great and glorious God takes an interest in little people like you and me. He even sent His Son, the Lord Jesus Christ, into the world to save all who put their trust in Him. And if you looked up John's Gospel, chapter three and verse sixteen, you will know that that is what that verse says!

22

God's Word Applied

"My sheep hear My voice, and I know them, and they follow Me."
John 10:27

All sorts and types of people went to hear Spurgeon preach—Christians, non-Christians, rich and poor, young and old. One day a Christian from outside London went to hear him, and as he arrived at the Metropolitan Tabernacle he looked round and was very surprised to see another man from his village going in to the church. He was surprised not so much to see someone he knew, but surprised to see this man there, because he wasn't the kind of person you might expect to go to listen to the Word of God being faithfully preached.

Of course, we ought to be pleased whenever anyone comes to hear God's message. Maybe they've never heard the gospel before, and they don't really understand why the Lord Jesus Christ died on the cross. Perhaps they've not had their sins forgiven, so they desperately need to understand the way of salvation. Many unsaved people went to hear Spurgeon, and he was very glad about that, and whenever he preached, he tried to challenge them about the salvation of their never-dying souls, and invite them to come to Christ.

Well, outside the Tabernacle the Christian went up to the other man and said, "I am surprised to see you here!" The man must have heard Spurgeon before, because he said, "Ah, every man has his own tale told here!"

He realized that God was speaking to him through Spurgeon's sermons, and that what was said applied to him. It seemed to him that God was saying that He knew all about him, the kind of life he had lived, the sins he had committed, his hopes and fears—everything was known to God!

God is still the same today, and He still speaks to us as we listen to His Word being explained. That is one of the reasons Christians go to church. They go to speak to God in prayer, to praise and thank Him, and to ask Him for what they need. But they also go to listen to Him speaking to them. It is two-way communication! We speak to Him in prayer, and He speaks to us in His Word.

God knows all about you: everything you have ever said or done—your whole situation—and He has something to say to you! Maybe it is about your sin, how you have disobeyed Him, how you are guilty in His sight. Maybe it is about His holiness, how He hates sin, and has to punish it. Maybe it is about the only way of escape—turning from your sin and trusting in His Son and His death upon the cross. Maybe it is about how to live a life that pleases Him day by day.

I wonder if you really expect God to speak to you when you go to church and listen to His Word being explained? Jesus said, *"My sheep hear My voice, and I know them, and they follow Me" (John 10:27)*. He knows His Own, He speaks to them, and they listen to what He has to say, and they follow Him.

23

What We REALLY Believe

"Now concerning the things which I write to you, indeed, before God, I do not lie."
Galatians 1:20

Now I'll tell you another story about two men who were friends. One day they met in the street. One was a Christian, and the other was an atheist. Do you know what an atheist is? It is someone who thinks that God doesn't exist! God made the world in which we live, and He made each one of us—but an atheist imagines that there is no God!

When they met, the atheist said to the Christian, "Where are you going?" The Christian replied, "To the Tabernacle! Where are you going?" The atheist said, "I'm going there, too!"

Now this was a surprise for the Christian. He hadn't expected his atheist friend would want to go and hear what Spurgeon had to say from the Bible, so he said, "You don't mean to say that you believe what Mr Spurgeon says?" The answer he got was very interesting: "No, but he does!"

The atheist realized that, although he didn't believe what was being preached, Spurgeon himself certainly did. He could tell that preaching the Word of God was not just a job for him, or merely something that he enjoyed doing. He preached the Bible because he really believed the Bible! He believed what it said, and especially what it said about the way of salvation.

Some people seem to imagine that the gospel message about the forgiveness of sins and the promise of heaven is just something to cheer us up and make us feel better. They think that it isn't necessarily true—in fact some people today say that, although they admire what the four Gospels tell us about Jesus, they don't believe that many of the things recorded about Him actually happened. They don't believe in the virgin birth (that Mary was His mother but Joseph wasn't His father because God's Holy Spirit was involved in His unique birth), or that Jesus performed all the wonderful miracles mentioned in the Gospels, or that when He died on the cross He was taking the punishment for the sins of all those who would trust in Him, or that after His death He rose again on the third day.

Can you think of some of the miracles Jesus performed?

- He turned ______________ into ______________.
- He stilled a ______________.
- He walked on ______________.
- He gave ______________ to the blind.
- He even raised the ______________ to life again.

All these are truths that Christians really believe. We are convinced that the Bible is honest and trustworthy. We don't just say those things—with all our hearts we believe them to be true! What the apostle Paul wrote to the Christians in Galatia can be applied to all the Bible: "*Now concerning the things which I write to you, indeed, before God, I do not lie*" *(Galatians 1:20).*

24

A Sermon for a Farmer

"I am the good Shepherd; and I know My sheep, and am known by My Own."
John 10:14

All preachers have to ask themselves before they speak, "What shall I preach about?" Of course, a faithful preacher will always preach from the Word of God, but there is so much in that Word! Spurgeon, who preached so often, was always asking himself, "What topic or verse from the Bible shall I preach from next?"

Spurgeon had two sons, Charles and Thomas, and when they were grown up, they both became preachers. On one occasion, Charles was going to speak at some special meetings in the countryside. He caught a train, and when he got off at the right station he found a horse and cart waiting to take him to the church where the meeting was to be held. The driver was a local farmer.

It wasn't long before the two of them started talking. The farmer said to Charles, "So you be Mr Spugen, be you, the son of the great man in Lunnon! I bin once in Lunnon, and 'eard 'im! I was up at the cattle show, and went over to 'is big chapel, and 'e preached about ... SHEEP! Bless you, 'e knew more about sheep then I do; and yet I've bin a farmer all me life!" He was talking in English, but the kind of English country folk sometimes speak! Perhaps you can put some of his mistakes right!

Spurgeon knew a great deal about lots of things, and the farmer confessed that he didn't know as much about sheep as Spurgeon did! I don't know exactly what was said in that sermon, but maybe you can think of some Bible verses that speak about sheep.

There is a verse that tells us that we are like sheep because we are very often silly and wander about and get lost—"All we like sheep have gone astray" (Isaiah 53:6). That's in the Old Testament, but the New Testament also contains references to sheep, and also to one particular Shepherd. It was the Lord Jesus Christ Who said, *"I am the good Shepherd; and I know My sheep, and am known by My Own" (John 10:14).* If we trust in Him, then He is our Shepherd, and a Shepherd Who cares for, looks after, and feeds His sheep.

I'm sure that you have seen flocks of sheep out in the fields, usually on their own and without a shepherd. Things were different all those years ago in Bible times. Then a shepherd would stay with his sheep, defending them against any wild animals that might be around, and against thieves and robbers. When the sheep had to move to fresh pastures the shepherd would go in front of them and lead the way, and if any did wander off, he would go and find them and bring them back. Think of the ways in which the Lord Jesus as the Good Shepherd does all those things for His sheep.

Here's something else you could do. Have a look in a hymn book and see how many hymns you can find about sheep and the Good Shepherd.

25

The Same Message

"For I determined not to know anything among you except Jesus Christ and Him crucified."
1 Corinthians 2:2

One Sunday, after Spurgeon had been the pastor at the Metropolitan Tabernacle for about twenty years, he recognized an American man in his congregation who had heard him preach many years before. Spurgeon said that the visitor would soon see that he was preaching the same old truths from the Bible as he had in years gone by. He hadn't begun by preaching Jesus and His cross and then gone on to something else. He was still preaching all about Jesus, all about the cross, all about forgiveness, all about faith or trust in the Lord.

Then Spurgeon told a story about a man who was well known in London in those days—Richard Cecil. One morning when Richard was a boy, his father took him to the city and told him to wait in a gateway for a while until he came back. Well, his father had many things to do and people to see, and was so busy that he completely forgot all about Richard!

The day went by, and in the evening the father went home. He was soon asked, "Where's Richard?"

Only then did he remember his son! "Dear me, I left him in the morning, standing under such-and-such a gateway, and I told him to stay there until I came back for him, and probably that is where he is now!"

So the father and others from his home rushed back to the city, and there, sure enough, was poor Richard, still waiting in that gateway!

Spurgeon, after telling this story, said that he was like young Richard. He had his orders from his Master, the Lord Jesus Christ, and he would stay where Jesus told him to stay, and go on preaching the same old truths from the Bible. He said, "It is of Christ I love to speak—Christ Who loved, and lived, and died, the Substitute for sinners, the Just for the unjust, that He might bring us to God!"

If you go to church or to Sunday School you will hear about God and Jesus, about the cross and sin week after week. Maybe you sometimes feel that you would like to hear something different, but the gospel message is the most important one you can ever hear, and also, even after a lifetime of hearing about these things, there will always be something more for you to learn. You might like to ask an elderly Christian, "Do you understand everything about the Lord Jesus Christ? Do you understand all the Bible?" You will soon discover that even the most mature Christian is still a learner, and that we can never know too much about the Saviour.

The apostle Paul had the right idea. He wrote, *"For I determined not to know anything among you except Jesus Christ and Him crucified" (1 Corinthians 2:2).*

26

Plain Words

"And my speech and my preaching were not with persuasive words of human wisdom, but in demonstration of the Spirit and of power."
1 Corinthians 2:4

Spurgeon was criticized by many people, and some said that he was coarse in the way he spoke—in other words, he didn't use flowery words. That was true. He didn't try to show off; instead, he spoke in language that people could readily understand. I expect you can guess why this was! He knew that he had something very important to say, because it concerned where his hearers would spend eternity, and so he wanted ordinary people to understand God's message.

To illustrate this, he told this story.

One day he got talking to a sailor, who told him that the captain of his ship was a real gentleman. He never used coarse or rough language. Well, one night, when the ship was at sea, the captain came on deck, and noticed three or four sailors who were up in the rigging playing cards by the light of a lantern. This was certainly not what the captain wanted to see! So he called out to them, "Aloft there, extinguish that luminator!" Can you understand what he meant?

The sailors took no notice. He called out again, "I say, extinguish that luminator!" They still took no notice! So he called out very loudly a third time, "Extinguish that luminator!"

But they went on playing cards! The captain by this time was getting rather cross! How dare they refuse to obey his orders? He went below and found the first mate, and told him that he had ordered these card-playing sailors to extinguish their luminator, but that they had taken no notice of him. He told him to go and get them, and he would have them punished for disobeying orders!

Can you guess why they didn't obey the captain's orders? Maybe you had the same trouble that they did! The first mate said, "Oh, sir, they did not understand you!" Did you understand him? If you didn't, here's a clue—imagine yourself holding a torch—now, can you 'extinguish that luminator'?

The first mate said to the captain, "I'll go and tell them!" So both of them went back on deck, and the first mate called out, "You there! Put out that light!" And the sailors did so immediately! They hadn't understood the captain's complicated words, but when the first mate gave them the same order in simple language, they understood straight away!

The apostle Paul knew how important it is to put things simply so that ordinary people can understand. He wrote, *"And my speech and my preaching were not with persuasive words of human wisdom, but in demonstration of the Spirit and of power" (1 Corinthians 2:4).*

God speaks plainly in His Word, especially about the way of salvation. If we turn from our sins and trust in the Lord Jesus Christ, our sins are forgiven, we have eternal life, and we will one day go to heaven.

27

Father and Son Preaching

"But as many as received Him, to them He gave the right to become children of God, even to those who believe in His name."
John 1:12

One day both Spurgeon and his son Charles were to preach in the East End of London, Spurgeon in the morning and younger Charles in the evening. On the way, they drove through Smithfield Meat Market, and saw all the meat there for sale. A little later they went through a very crowded part of the city, and, still thinking of what they had seen in the Market, they talked about the fact that just as our bodies need food, so do our souls. Meat for our bodies, and the Word of God for our souls!

The church that had organized this occasion owned quite a small building, so they had borrowed a much bigger one for the meetings, but, even so, well before the first service was due to start it was quite full with people, and many more were still outside, wanting to get in! When Spurgeon went up into the pulpit, hundreds remained outside, so he had an idea. He turned to Charles and asked whether he would be willing to preach in a church which was just opposite, and Charles agreed.

Spurgeon told the people to tell those outside "that his dear son Charles would preach just over the way, in the Baptist Chapel." So everyone was able to hear one of the two Spurgeons!

But what about the evening meeting? Charles was due to preach at that, and again the large building was full up and people were outside wanting to get in! So he copied his father, and asked him if he would preach in a schoolroom over the road, which he did. So the two Spurgeons preached opposite each other morning and evening—the younger one taking the overflow meeting for the older one in the morning, and the older one taking the overflow meeting for the younger one in the evening!

On the way back Spurgeon said, "Well, Charlie, I do not suppose it has ever happened before, that a father and son should be preaching opposite to one another at the same time; but, thank God, dear boy, not in opposition!"

In fact, the same thing happened again later—this time in Pollockshaws which is part of Glasgow in Scotland, but with a difference. A thousand people heard Spurgeon preach, and Charles had to take the overflow service—but three or four thousand people attended his meeting! There were many more in the overflow meeting than in the main meeting! And Spurgeon was so happy that his son had a bigger congregation than he did! Afterwards, thousands stayed around, blocking the road, and shaking hands with both father and son—and cheering them loudly when they left!

Spurgeon was delighted that both his sons, Charles and Thomas, were believers in the Lord Jesus Christ, and also that they became preachers of the gospel. So they were in the same physical and spiritual family as their father. Do you know how people become members of God's family? The apostle John explains this to us: *"But as many as received Him (the Lord Jesus), to them He gave the right to become children of God, even to those who believe in His name" (John 1:12)*. If we trust in Jesus, then we are in God's spiritual family.

28

How to Be the Greatest Preacher in the World

"Holding fast the faithful word ..."
Titus 1:9

Maybe you have visited different towns and cities, and perhaps you have been abroad. When people go to a new place, they want to see interesting and special sites. Here's a list of some cities, with their famous attractions, but they are jumbled up. See if you can draw a line from each city to its right attraction. (Use a pencil, not a pen, so you can rub it out later.)

Athens	Tower Bridge
Edinburgh	Holyrood House
London	Eiffel Tower
Paris	Colosseum
Rome	Areopagus

Can you think of any famous places that bring visitors to London? There is Buckingham Palace, the Tower of London, Nelson's Column, and plenty of others—including one mentioned above!

In Spurgeon's day, people came from all over the world to visit London, although not, of course, as many as today. Travel was much slower then, and no one could fly to Heathrow or Gatwick Airport! People from other countries had to come by ship.

On one occasion a boy, aged eight, came with his father from America. Where should they go? What places should they visit? I expect they went to the sites we've already mentioned, but they also put another on their list—the Metropolitan Tabernacle to hear Spurgeon! The father told his son they were going to hear the greatest preacher in the world, which would have sounded very exciting!

It must have been quite a sight and experience to go into the Tabernacle and see all the thousands of people there! And then Spurgeon entered the pulpit and the service began. The boy leaned forward with his mouth open, and listened throughout the whole meeting, hardly taking his eyes off 'the greatest preacher in the world'.

Afterwards, when they were outside in the street, the father asked, "Willie, what do you think of that man?" The boy replied, "Is that the greatest preacher in the world?" "Yes," the father answered, "I think he is!" Willie said, "Well, then, I know how to be the greatest preacher in the world!" "How?" asked his father. "Why, just pick out a nice chapter in the Bible, and tell just what is in it so that everybody can understand you, and nothing more!"

And that is preaching, good preaching—telling just what the Bible says so that everybody can understand it, and nothing more! The apostle Paul told Titus what he wanted preachers to do: *"Holding fast the faithful word as he has been taught, that he may be able, by sound doctrine, both to exhort and convict those who contradict" (Titus 1:9).*

29

Pickpocket!

"... they hear your words, but they do not do them ..."
Ezekiel 33:31

The Metropolitan Tabernacle was a very large building, and inside at the front was a big platform rather than a pulpit. Usually as Spurgeon preached, the deacons sat behind him. One Sunday he was preaching, when, quite suddenly, he did something that maybe not everyone noticed. Just for a second or two he said something very quietly to the deacons. Certainly the rest of the people didn't hear what he said. And then he carried on with his sermon.

Well, I can tell you what he said. It was, "Pickpocket! Mrs So-and-so's pew!" And that was all!

What had happened was this. In the middle of his sermon, with thousands of people there, Spurgeon had noticed one man picking someone's pocket—that is, stealing from that person!

Two of the deacons immediately and quietly left their seats, and went down the stairs behind the platform. They went out of the church through the back door and round to the front, where there was a policeman on duty. They reported what Spurgeon had seen, and then all three entered the church, walked down to the pew Spurgeon had indicated, and arrested the pickpocket!

Did you realize that preachers see what is going on in church? They can see if people are following the Bible reading, if they are interested in what is being said, if they are paying attention! It is very discouraging for a preacher to feel that his congregation has no real interest in God's message. On the other hand, he will be encouraged if he sees people eager to listen and enthusiastic to learn more about the Lord Jesus.

More important than the preacher seeing you is the fact that God Himself sees you. He sees you all the time, of course, wherever you are. He sees if, when you go to church or to Sunday School, you are interested in what He has to say to you through His word.

Ezekiel was a preacher and a prophet, who had a very difficult time. He was called upon to preach to people who really didn't want to hear God's message. Almost at the beginning of his prophetic ministry the Lord warned him that he was being sent to a rebellious people, but Ezekiel was faithful despite the many problems that faced him. Later, God said to him, *"So they come to you as people do, they sit before you as My people, and they hear your words, but they do not do them; for with their mouth they show much love, but their hearts pursue their own gain" (Ezekiel 33:31)*. There they sat, listening to the prophet, and maybe after the sermon they might have said, "Mr Ezekiel, thank you for your sermon this morning! It was wonderful!" They heard, but they did not obey. They said nice words, but inside they were rebellious. And, knowing what they were like, as he looked round his congregation, Ezekiel must have been very sad!

May you be an encouragement to those who teach you God's truth, and, most of all, may you please the Lord Who has been so good to you!

30

Old Skinflints!

"God loves a cheerful giver."
2 Corinthians 9:7

Now, here's a test for you—don't turn the pages of this book back yet—what were the first few stories about? The first was entitled, "Something More To Do"—what was that something more that Spurgeon wanted his church to do and to get involved with? Here's a clue if you've forgotten—it had something to do with children. And here's another clue—these children didn't have anyone to look after them. I expect you remember now—it was to start an orphanage!

You might also remember from my second book, that Spurgeon started a college to train men who wanted to serve the Lord, but who didn't have a very good education or maybe couldn't afford to pay for training. There were many other things that he and the church were involved with—books were sent to pastors who couldn't afford to buy them and there was the home for elderly people, too.

What was needed to keep all these things going? I'm sure you know—money! Spurgeon himself gave a great deal of his own money to enable these good works to continue, but, of course, he expected other Christians to give as well. If we love the Lord we will give what we can to help others and to ensure that many people hear the gospel message.

On one occasion, Spurgeon spoke at a meeting. I don't know where, but it was not in his own church. At the end he said, "I am now going to pass round my hat for a collection towards the upkeep of the Orphanage, and the College, and the other good works that we do."

So it was that Spurgeon's hat was passed round the congregation, and, of course, eventually it got back to him. He looked in it. You would never guess how much was in it! Nothing! The hat was absolutely empty! No one had given anything!

Spurgeon must have been disappointed, not for his own sake, but for the sake of the orphans and the college students and others, too, who would have benefited from any money given.

He said, "Let us pray. I thank Thee, O Lord, that at least these old skinflints have given me my hat back!"

If you know the Lord Jesus, you know that He gave the most precious thing He had for you—His Own life! He gave up heaven for you when He came to this world, and on the cross He sacrificed Himself to pay the price for your sins. He gave His all! And He has continued to give you many good things. Every day He gives you good gifts. You cannot ever fully repay Him for His gifts, but at least you can give some things to Him—your life and your service, and, as you are able, some money, too! The apostle Paul wrote, *"God loves a cheerful giver" (2 Corinthians 9:7).*

31

Mrs Bartlett

"Jesus said, 'Let the little children come to Me'."
Matthew 19:14

Maybe you go to Sunday School, but I don't think that you've ever been to a Sunday School like the one in this story!

You might remember that before the Metropolitan Tabernacle was built, the church met in New Park Street Chapel, and that is where Spurgeon began his ministry in London. About five years after he started there, the church had an afternoon Sunday School. It so happened that one of the teachers was going away for a month, so she had to find a replacement for her girls' class. She asked a lady called Mrs Lavinia Bartlett to fill in for her.

So it was that one Sunday Mrs Bartlett went to take the senior class, but there were only three girls in it! Undaunted, she taught them God's truth as best she could for all the Sundays of that month. The wonderful thing was that week by week the numbers attending increased! At the end of the month, things were going so well that she was asked to stay on as a teacher. And that is what she did—she stayed on—and on—and on!

Before long the class was too big to fit into the room where they met. After ten years there were five hundred in her class! When the Tabernacle was opened, Mrs Bartlett's class met in one of the big halls there, and by then usually six or seven hundred girls were coming!

Often she wasn't at all well, but she carried on with the work. She had started teaching thinking that she would only be in that class for a month, but by the time she died she had taught there for sixteen years! Of course, she was not the only teacher in the Sunday School. In Spurgeon's day there were about one hundred teachers and over a thousand boys and girls!

Why do you think that Mrs Bartlett taught in that Sunday School? What did she want for the children who went there?

Yes, she wanted each one to get to know and love and follow the Lord Jesus Christ. Her prayers were wonderfully answered, for in those sixteen years, between nine hundred and a thousand members of the class became believers! If you go to Sunday School, that is what your teacher wants for you!

On one occasion, some little children were brought to Jesus but His disciples didn't think that this was a good idea at all! They tried to turn the children away. *"But Jesus said, 'Let the little children come to Me, and do not forbid them; for of such is the kingdom of heaven'" (Matthew 19:14).* Jesus welcomes all who come to Him, no matter how young they are!

32

The ABC Gospel

"Come to Me ... and I will give you rest."
Matthew 11:28

In the last story we thought about Mrs Bartlett's Bible class. Every year they had a special tea and meeting. One year she asked a young man called Manton Smith to speak to the girls.

The day came and Manton arrived, but then he got an awful shock because Spurgeon himself came into the hall where the meeting was to be held! He had been asked to be the chairman. I think Manton was nervous enough speaking to all those people, but with Spurgeon there as well ... ! He thought to himself, "How ever am I going to speak in front of Mr Spurgeon?"

I think that Spurgeon must have noticed that Manton was very nervous, and he tried to cheer him up and encourage him. Manton later said, "How I stood I cannot tell, for the trembling of my legs I shall never forget!" But up he stood, despite his shaking legs and his nerves, and said, "I am a bad speaker and a worse writer, and all is know is the ABC gospel."

To Manton's surprise, Spurgeon rapped his stick on the floor and knocked his hat on the table, and said, "Bravo, go on, brother! That is just the sort of gospel I like! Tell us about it!"

So Manton told all the people the ABC gospel. I wonder

if you can guess what he had in mind. Well, I'll give you a clue—he was thinking about Bible quotations that begin with the letters A, B and C. Can you think of any before you read on? Maybe they are the ones that he had in mind.

For A he chose, "All have sinned and come short of the glory of God." That's found in Paul's letter to the Romans, chapter 3 verse 23.

For B he quoted John the Baptist, "Behold! The Lamb of God Who takes away the sin of the world!" John, in his Gospel, records that in chapter 1 and verse 29.

Lastly, for C he chose one of the most wonderful things that Jesus ever said. It is His gracious and genuine invitation—*"Come to Me, all you who labor and are heavy laden, and I will give you rest." Matthew* tells us about that in chapter *11* verse *28*.

I'm sure that he then explained how all of us are sinners, how the Lord Jesus came to deal with sin, and how we are all invited to go to Him and find forgiveness and salvation through Him.

Manton got to the end of his talk, and quite expected Spurgeon to be disgusted and maybe even ashamed of him. He felt himself to be a very poor speaker, especially compared to the great preacher. But he was in for another surprise. He turned to look at Spurgeon, and saw tears rolling down his face! He had been affected by the simple explanation of the gospel Manton had made, shook him by the hand, and said, "God bless you, my young brother! Stick to that kind of talk, and you will be a real ABC, which I consider stands for Able-Bodied Christian!"

33

A Fly on the Nose!

"The entrance of Your words gives light; it gives understanding to the simple."
Psalm 119:130

Occasionally you meet some funny people in churches—not in the one you go to, I'm sure—but I want to tell you about a rather strange man one speaker had in his congregation.

This preacher later became the pastor of a church in Glasgow in Scotland, but early on in his preaching career, as a young man, he went to a particular church to take the service. He looked round the congregation and saw one man sitting near the front doing something very strange. This man was one of the officers of the church, and you'd never guess what he was doing. He sat there with his fingers in his ears! I'm sure I don't know why he did this—I suppose that he just didn't like the young preacher and didn't want to hear what he had to say!

I'll tell you a little later about someone who wanted to hear preaching, but couldn't because he was deaf. This man had the opposite problem—he could hear but didn't want to!

What could the preacher do? I don't know what I'd do in that situation, and this young preacher didn't know what to do either. Anyway, he carried on with the service while the man sat there with his ears stuffed with his fingers!

Later on, the young man told Spurgeon about this strange

incident. He wondered if Spurgeon had any advice to give him if he found himself in a similar situation—not that he was likely to! He said, "There was a nice thing for a young preacher! What would you have done, Mr Spurgeon?"

"I should have prayed ..." began Spurgeon—and the young man put a solemn look on his face because he was expecting something very spiritual. Well, what do you think that Spurgeon would have prayed?

"Yes," he said, "I should have prayed that a fly might have landed on his nose!"

If Spurgeon had been the preacher, and his prayer had been answered, I'm sure that you can work out what would have happened!

You don't need to put your fingers in your ears not to hear though, do you? If you don't concentrate on what is being said, you won't hear and understand. God's voice in the Bible is the most important voice to listen to.

The Psalmist in the longest Psalm said this: *"The entrance of Your words gives light; it gives understanding to the simple" (Psalm 119:130)*. If God's Word is to enter your heart your ears must be open, and your heart, too!

34

The Man Who Couldn't Hear

"Not forsaking the assembling of ourselves together, as is the manner of some."
Hebrews 10:25

Well, the last story was about a man who could hear, but didn't want to. Now for a story about a man with the opposite problem.

For many years, every Sunday morning as he went to the Metropolitan Tabernacle, one of Spurgeon's friends would meet an elderly Christian gentleman going to his own church. And each time they met, the old man would strike his hand upon his breast, and say, "Good morning! I've got him here, sir!"

What do you think he meant? That was, of course, what Spurgeon's friend wondered, too! He came to the conclusion that the old man was referring to the Lord Jesus Christ, Whom he had in his heart. We become Christians by asking Jesus into our hearts, and He comes in to save, rule and to look after us.

Eventually, however, he found out that he had been wrong. It turned out that the old gentleman was very deaf, and was unable to hear a word his pastor said! But, being a Christian, he enjoyed meeting with the Lord's people, feeling a part of his church, and I'm sure he worshipped the Lord even though he couldn't follow any of the prayers or hear anything that was going on.

The members of the church knew about his deafness, so they always found the right hymns for him so that he was able to think about the words even though he couldn't hear the singing. Likewise, they found the Bible readings for him, and he could read that for himself. But what would he do during the sermon? Well, every Sunday he put one of Spurgeon's sermons in his breast pocket, and while the pastor preached a sermon he couldn't hear, he would read Spurgeon's sermon to himself! I don't know, but maybe he read a better sermon than the one spoken in his own church!

So Spurgeon's friend was wrong—the old man when he said, "I've got him here, sir," wasn't referring to the Lord Jesus, but to Spurgeon's sermon! But, of course, he had Jesus in his heart, too—Jesus in his heart and the sermon near his heart!

If you go to church, you ought to try to gain as much as you can from being there, but even if you can't get as much as you would like, or as much as others, it is important to meet with the Lord's people. That elderly man knew that.

The writer of the letter to the Hebrews gave his readers—and us—this advice and instruction: *"Not forsaking the assembling of ourselves together, as is the manner of some, but exhorting one another, and so much the more as you see the Day approaching" (Hebrews 10:25)*. In other words, continue to meet together with the Lord's people to worship Him and to listen to Him.

35

Christ or Business

"... if you confess with your mouth the Lord Jesus ..."
Romans 10:9

There was a man who was the manager of a large brewery, which is a place where alcoholic drinks are made. He became a Christian—trusting in Jesus Christ—but, despite that, he wasn't at all happy! He started to read Spurgeon's sermons every week, hoping that they might cheer him up, but they didn't. In fact they made him feel more miserable. Can you work out why that was? Most Christians found Spurgeon's sermons very helpful—but there he was, getting more and more unhappy!

It was because he saw from what Spurgeon said that if he was really going to live the Christian life, Jesus Christ must be not only his Saviour and Friend, but also something else. What is that? Think about this verse, and pick out the one word which answers that question: "*... if you confess with your mouth the Lord Jesus and believe in your heart that God has raised Him from the dead, you will be saved" (Romans 10:9).*

Yes, the word is 'Lord'. Jesus must be your Lord. That means full surrender. It means that you do what He wants and not what you want. It means that He is your Master, the One you obey.

So why was the man so miserable? Because he knew that he wasn't pleasing Jesus by being the manager of that brewery.

He understood that all through the history of the world, lives have been ruined through drinking alcohol. The Bible tells us that it is a sin to get drunk. So often one drink leads to another which leads to another, and people who have too much to drink get into all kinds of trouble. And drinking alcohol is addictive—that means that once you start, it is very difficult to stop. The best thing to do is never to start! Alcohol can (and does) kill many people, and causes untold misery to family and friends.

So here was this man, claiming to be a Christian and yet working as the manager of a brewery! No wonder he was so unhappy!

He knew that he had to make a choice—his job or Jesus. He decided that he must follow Jesus. So he told his uncle, who was the big boss in the brewery, that he had to give up his job, and told him why. His uncle and also his father thought he was being very foolish and tried to persuade him not to leave and not to throw away what they thought was his only chance in life to be successful. But he said, "I must throw away this or Christ: the one I cannot, the business I must!" His uncle then offered to give him as many shares in the brewery as he wanted, which would have made him very rich, but he still said, "No!" So he left, not knowing where he would go, or what he would do, but trusting the Lord. It wasn't very long afterwards that he became a City Missionary, and the Lord used him in telling others about the way of salvation.

If Jesus is to be your Saviour, He must be your Lord, too, and sometimes you will have to decide between Him and other things. If you are a real Christian, you must put Him first.

36

Get After That Man!

"... everyone who believes is justified from all things ..."
Acts 13:39

Spurgeon had many helpers in his church, not only elders and deacons. Many others helped the work forward in different ways, and I want to tell you about two men and what they did. They would go out into the streets around the Tabernacle to witness to people, invite them to the services and give out tracts. One of these men had been a famous runner, and had won prizes in many races! Usually every Sunday morning they would go out on opposite sides of the same street.

One morning one of the men gave a tract to a man who said, "What is the use of giving me this tract? I shall be in hell in an hour!"

The other Christian man crossed the road to join his friend and said to him, "Did you hear what that man said?" "No," said his friend, "what was it?" "He looked very wild," was the reply, "and talked of being in hell in an hour! He is either mad, or he is going to commit suicide!" Said the other, "Come on, let's follow him!"

So they caught up with the man, and one asked him, "What did you say when you took that tract?" He replied, "That is no concern of yours! Mind your own business!" The Christian said, "Oh, but it is my business, for, if I heard you aright, you said that you would be in hell in an hour." The man said,

"Yes, that is what I said, and I'll be out of this world in an hour!" Then the Christian said, "No you won't, for I mean to stick by you, and I won't leave you for an hour, wherever you go!"

Well, then the man started telling the Christians a bit about himself. He hadn't eaten anything for three days, and had walked the streets all night! So they gave him a good breakfast, and then took him to church. After that, they took him to where they usually had dinner and he ate with them. In the afternoon, they took him to the Bible class, and again to church in the evening. And, wonderfully, he was converted!

Then he told his two new friends more about himself. He had lived a wicked life, although his wife was a Christian. They had lived in the North of England, but four or five months earlier he had left her and come to London. Before long, the Christians paid his fare home and he went back to his home. His wife was very pleased to see him again, and especially glad that he, too, was now a believer!

She wrote to the two Christian men, telling them that she had prayed for her husband for a long time, but after he left her she thought that she would never see him again. Now she was so happy and thankful to the Lord, and also to those two Christians who went after him that Sunday morning.

God put things right in that man's life, because He put the man right! And He will do the same for everyone who trusts in Him. The Bible says, *"And by Him (the Lord Jesus) everyone who believes is justified from all things" (Acts 13:39).*

37

Blow Up the Tabernacle!

"... and fell down on his face at His feet, giving Him thanks ..."
Luke 17:16

Not very far off the west coast of England is a beautiful island called Ireland. If you look closely at a map, you will see that it is divided into two. Part of the north is Northern Ireland which is in the United Kingdom, and the rest is the Republic of Ireland, which is a completely separate country.

A few years ago, there was a lot of trouble and fighting in Northern Ireland. Some people wanted that part of Ireland to join the Republic and others wanted it to stay within the United Kingdom. Sadly, many people were injured or killed. The Irish Republican Army set off bombs not only in Northern Ireland, but also in London and other places in England. Even in Spurgeon's day there was a lot of trouble over Ireland, not caused by the Irish Republican Army, but by a group called the Fenians.

In 1884, it was decided to hold some special meetings at the Tabernacle to celebrate the fact that Spurgeon had been the church's pastor for thirty years. Many people were expected to attend. But just then there was a warning that the Fenians were going to cause trouble in London. They were threatening to blow up the Metropolitan Tabernacle on the very night that a large meeting was to be held there! It was decided that the service should go ahead, but in the congregation were a great number of policemen and detectives. They must have been looking round at all the people, on the lookout for anyone acting suspiciously. That must have been very difficult for them because there were about five and a half thousand people at the meeting!

The service went well, and thankfully there was no trouble, so the threats of the Fenians came to nothing. Spurgeon had not been told of the possibility of people trying to blow up the Tabernacle, because no one wanted to worry him unduly, but his wife, Susannah, knew all about it. On the way home in their carriage, she told him. Guess what they both did? Together they gave thanks to the Lord that everybody had been kept safe.

When the Lord Jesus was here, He worked many wonderful miracles. On one occasion ten lepers came to Him and asked that He might be merciful to them. He told them to go to the priests, and on their way they were healed! But the sad thing was this: only one came back to Jesus, *"and fell down on his face at His feet, giving Him thanks" (Luke 17:16).* Jesus said, I'm sure with sadness, "Were there not ten cleansed? But where are the nine?" (verse 17). You can read the story in Luke's Gospel, chapter 17 verses 11–19.

I'm sure your parents have told you to say, "Thank you" when somebody gives you something. God has given you so much—so thank Him!

38

Nice Boots!

"Come, buy and eat ... without money and without price."
Isaiah 55:1

One day a beggar knocked at Spurgeon's door. In those days there were many very poor people in Britain, especially in the big cities. Well, of course, Spurgeon felt sorry for him, and wanted to help him in some way.

I wonder why the beggar had chosen to knock at that particular house? Maybe he knew something about Spurgeon which made him feel that he would receive a sympathetic hearing and some help—after all, Spurgeon was known as a believer in the Lord Jesus Christ who tried to show Christian love and compassion to all kinds of people. However, it is possible that the beggar may have seen a list ... Some years later, the police in London found a professional beggar's handbook listing the names of people likely to give help to those in need. Guess whose name was first on the list? Yes, Spurgeon's!

Anyway, there was this beggar, and one thing that Spurgeon noticed was that he needed some new shoes. Either the ones he was wearing were in a very poor state—maybe they were falling to pieces and not at all comfortable—or maybe he hadn't got any on at all! Spurgeon felt that he had to do something about it, so he gave the man a pair of patent leather boots. Lovely they were, and the beggar put them on then and there, and they fitted him perfectly! He was very pleased, and thanked Spurgeon a lot! So off he went, extremely happy.

Quite a bit later on, Spurgeon saw this same beggar. He looked down at the man's feet, expecting to see the nice boots—but the man wasn't wearing them!

"Where are the boots I gave you?" Spurgeon asked.

Now, before I tell you what the beggar's answer was, try to think why he wasn't wearing the boots. Remember the kind of footwear they were, and what the man was trying to get from people. Have you worked it out?

The man in reply said something like this, "Well, I liked the boots, and they were very comfortable. But when I went begging, people saw the boots and said to themselves, 'He doesn't look as though he needs any money if he can go around in those expensive boots!' And nobody gave me anything. So when I go begging I have to go without the boots!"

Spurgeon later used this as an illustration, and pointed out that it is like that when we go to the Lord Jesus Christ. We are like beggars; we have no goodness of our own. We have to take off our own self-righteousness, our supposed goodness, and we have to come to Him in all our need, just as we are. The Lord's invitation is *"Come, buy and eat. Yes, come, buy wine and milk without money and without price" (Isaiah 55:1)*. As the hymn puts it: 'Just as I am and waiting not, to rid my soul of one dark blot, to Thee Whose blood can cleanse each spot, O Lamb of God, I come.'

39

Crossing the Road

"You will guide me with Your counsel."
Psalm 73:24

You might remember that Spurgeon was born in a village in Essex, called Kelvedon. He also spent quite a long time staying with his grandparents in Stambourne, another small place. The first church he pastored was in Waterbeach in Cambridgeshire, again a small town, although at different times he lived in both Colchester and Cambridge. But really he was used to country life and not city life.

The first time he went to London to preach, he didn't like it at all—the horses and carriages and noise and busyness. Maybe, if you have been brought up in a village or small town, when you visit a big city you feel a little bewildered. It can be very confusing!

One thing that Spurgeon never got to like was crossing a busy road! Today, of course, in a city you will see many types of vehicles going along the crowded streets—cars, taxis, motorbikes, buses, lorries, etc. In Spurgeon's day there weren't things like that, but there were carriages of various kinds pulled by horses. I dare say that it is quicker to stop a modern vehicle than a horse-drawn one! So crossing the road has always been dangerous. That is why you must obey the Highway Code. Do you know the Green Cross Code?

One day, Spurgeon was right in the middle of London—near the Bank of England. Have you seen that big building?

He wanted to cross the road—but he was too afraid to do so! I remember that I had a similar experience when I was in the capital of the Philippines—a city called Manila. I was with some Christian Filipinos, and they were used to crossing the road there—but I wasn't! There were six lanes of traffic all going in the same direction at great speed. Just like Spurgeon, I couldn't pluck up the courage to get across! In the end one of the Filipino girls came back and took me by the hand. I closed my eyes, and she led me safely across!

Well, there was Spurgeon wondering what he would do, when, of all things, a blind man came along, caught him by the arm and asked for help to cross the road!

"I am afraid to cross!" Spurgeon explained.

"But you can see!" said the blind man.

"Oh yes," Spurgeon replied. "I can see, but I am afraid!"

The man said, "If you can see, I'll trust you."

The blind man's trust gave Spurgeon the courage he needed, and so, arm in arm, the two men went safely across the road. When they got to the other side, the blind man said, "I knew I could trust you!"

It can be dangerous crossing roads, but it can be more dangerous travelling through life. How can anyone get safely to heaven? The answer is in what the blind man said to Spurgeon: "I knew I could trust you." We have to trust the Lord Jesus Christ. We will be safe if we are with Him. The Psalmist said, *"You will guide me with Your counsel, and afterwards receive me to glory" (Psalm 73:24).*

40

How Much Does Membership Cost?

"Your money perish with you,
because you thought that the gift of God
could be purchased with money!"
Acts 8:20

Every church has a membership—that is, people actually join and become members so that they can take their full part in all the work and witness of the church. It was just the same in the Metropolitan Tabernacle, and Spurgeon himself would usually interview those who wanted to join. But not everyone can join a church. What do you think is the first and main qualification?

I expect you know! Every person who joins a church should be a real Christian, someone who has been converted, who has been born again, who knows Jesus Christ as his or her own personal Lord and Saviour, and is following Him.

One day a man came to see Spurgeon, and said that he wanted to join the church. But as they talked it became clear that he wasn't trusting the Lord Jesus, and he wasn't a true Christian.

The man then offered to give £700 to any work connected with the church if Spurgeon would accept him as a member. Now that, even today, is a lot of money, but, of course, in those days it was worth much more! "I'll give it to the church, or to the College, or to the Orphanage—whatever you like!" Now what do you think of that generous offer?

Spurgeon said, "No!"

The man said, "But I'm offering you all this money just to become a member!"

Spurgeon replied, "No, not even if you offered me seventy times £700!"

I wonder why that man was so keen on joining. Can you think of any reasons? Was it because the Metropolitan Tabernacle was a very famous and popular church, and he wanted to do what many other people were doing? Perhaps he thought that he had great gifts which could be used. Or maybe he believed that becoming a member would ensure him a place in heaven.

Well, the years went by—and then this same man came to see Spurgeon again. He actually thanked him for refusing to have him as a member, because, he said, that had made him think deeply about spiritual things. He realized, through being refused membership, that he wasn't really a Christian at all. But, wonderfully, eventually he was converted, and then he did join the Tabernacle!

There is a very sad story in the Book of Acts about a man called Simon who thought that he could buy spiritual powers. *"But Peter said to him, 'Your money perish with you, because you thought that the gift of God could be purchased with money!'" (Acts 8:20)*. You cannot purchase salvation, nor can you buy your way into the membership of Christ's church. Salvation is a free gift—which is wonderful to know!

41

Honesty Is the Best Policy

"... in all things desiring to live honorably."
Hebrews 13:18

People who have different jobs need different tools. Can you draw an imaginary line from each person in the first column to the tool he or she would need?

A carpenter		books
A driver		a computer
A gardener	NEEDS	a saw
An IT specialist		a spade
A preacher		a vehicle

I'm sure that you worked out what a preacher needs! He may have a computer and a saw and a spade and a vehicle—but he must have books! The one that is always top of his list is, of course, the Bible, but he also needs other books to help him to understand the Scriptures better. You have probably got quite a few books, and so have I, but I don't suppose we have got as many as Spurgeon had. He had about 12,000! That's a huge number, and I think that he managed to read most if not all of them and, amazingly, he could remember much of what he had read!

You have probably got a favourite book (apart from the Bible!), and so had Spurgeon. One he liked a great deal—which you, too, may have read—was called *Pilgrim's Progress* by John Bunyan. However, the book that he called "the richest book in my library" was entitled *Things New and Old*, written by a man called John Spenser. It was very old—in fact, it was written in 1658!

This book had been given to him by a man he didn't know very well, who was called Mr Oliver. Spurgeon was very pleased with it, although it was in a rather poor state. After all those years, I'm not surprised! Now, Mr Oliver was eventually accused of some crimes, and Spurgeon discovered that the book he so much liked hadn't belonged to Mr Oliver at all—he had either stolen or borrowed it, and then given it to Spurgeon!

What should Spurgeon do? He found the book so helpful, and didn't want to part with it. I don't know if he was tempted to keep it, but he knew what the right thing to do was. He found out who it really belonged to, and he gave it back to its rightful owner. But he was sorry to lose the book!

However, soon afterwards, a Christian man—without knowing how much Spurgeon was missing the book—sent him another copy and this one was in far better condition than the one he had given back!

There is an old saying, 'Honesty is the best policy.' That is what the Lord tells us to be—honest and trustworthy. The writer of the letter to the Hebrews said, *"Pray for us; for we are confident that we have a good conscience, in all things desiring to live honorably" (Hebrews 13:18).*

42

Time and Eternity

"Lay up for yourselves treasures in heaven."
Matthew 6:20

As I'm sure you know by now, the Metropolitan Tabernacle was a very large building. At the front there was a big pulpit, more like a platform. What do you think might be in the pulpit? For one thing, I'm certain there was a Bible there. All preachers need a Bible! But there was something else, something that a speaker finds very useful—here's a clue: it stops him from preaching for too long! Can you guess?

In Spurgeon's pulpit there was a clock! Maybe there is one in the church you go to—if so, whereabouts is it?

Some while ago, I read a story about a lady from Asia who went to live in America, and one Sunday morning she attended a service in a church there. Afterwards, someone asked her how she had liked the meeting. She said, "I found it interesting! I have seen people worship many objects, but it's the first time I ever saw people worship a clock! During the sermon they all watched the clock with adoring eyes, and then when the two hands got together on the figure twelve, they all closed their eyes and prayed, and then the service was over. I've never seen clock worshippers before!"

When you are in church, try to concentrate on what is being said, and don't keep looking at the clock or your watch. You are not there to think about what time it is, or how soon the service will be over, but about much more important things. And I'm sure that the people at the Tabernacle were not clock worshippers!

So there was this clock in the Tabernacle pulpit, but a thief came along one day and stole it! Not only that, but another clock which was used in one of the church halls for the prayer meetings was stolen, too! The theft was reported in the media, and one newspaper claimed that the thief had a good excuse for stealing the clock—which was that Spurgeon was less concerned with time than with eternity!

It wasn't long before two people each gave a clock to replace the ones that were stolen, so Spurgeon could make sure that the services and prayer meetings didn't go on too long!

In His Sermon on the Mount, Jesus said, *"Do not lay up for yourselves treasures on earth, where moth and rust destroy and where thieves break in and steal; but lay up for yourselves treasures in heaven, where neither moth nor rust destroys and where thieves do not break in and steal" (Matthew 6:19–20).* Time is very short compared to eternity! Remember that when a church service seems to be going on for a long time, and try to think about where you will be spending eternity and whether you are ready to face God.

43
Travelling through Life

"Show me Your ways, O LORD."
Psalm 25:4

Spurgeon's sermons were full of everyday illustrations. In teaching truth in this way he copied the Lord Jesus Christ Himself. The people Jesus spoke to, for example, would often see sheep and shepherds—so He would speak about them. Can you think of anything He said about sheep? He once told a parable about a sheep that was what? Lost! He said that His followers are in some senses like sheep, and that He was the good Shepherd of His flock.

People also knew about weddings, so Jesus told a parable about a wedding feast, and of one man who went to it but had something missing. It was a wedding garment! Jesus spoke of so many other familiar items and events that His hearers would know a lot about. Can you think of any more?

When Spurgeon lived and worked in London, it was a bustling place, as it is today, of course. The streets were very busy with traffic. If you had wanted to travel somewhere, how would you have done so if you didn't have your own transport? Well, if you had enough money, you could travel by cab or taxi, and if you were a little poorer you could go by bus. Of course, in those days cabs and buses were drawn by horses.

But there was another mode of transport you could have used. Do you know what that might have been? You can still ride on them in a few places today, such as in Blackpool and Sheffield. Yes, you could have travelled by tram. Trams ran on rails like a train, but they went along the streets in towns and cities.

Spurgeon gave this illustration. He said that when the tramcar driver sets out on his journey, he goes straight ahead on the rails. If he could see all the route in front of him, he would see carts and carriages and buses and people blocking his way, and then he could say, "I'll never get to the end of the line with all those things on the tramline!" But he doesn't think like that. He just goes on, and when he sees something in his way, he will blow his whistle, the vehicle in front will get off the rails, and he will reach his destination.

Then he explained that the Christian life is like that. Between us and heaven there are so many obstacles, that if we thought of them all we might become afraid and despair. But all we need to do is just keep going straight on with the Lord, and when something gets in our way, we ought to sound the whistle of prayer and ask the Lord to help us. If we do that, we shall get safely to glory.

Although David the Psalmist didn't know anything about trams, he knew a lot about travelling through life with the Lord. He wrote, *"Show me Your ways, O LORD; teach me Your paths. Lead me in Your truth and teach me, for You are the God of my salvation; on You I wait all the day" (Psalm 25:4–5).*

44

Birthdays

"He who believes in the Son has everlasting life."
John 3:36

I like celebrating birthdays, don't you? It's nice to get some cards, and presents as well! Someone said that birthdays are good for you, because statistics show that the people who have the most of them live the longest! I'm sure that you know when your own birthday is. Maybe you know someone else who was also born on the same day as you were.

A couple of Sundays before Spurgeon's fiftieth birthday, after the morning service, a lady came up to him and told him that she was born on the very same day that he was, 19th June, 1834, and so she was looking forward to her fiftieth birthday later that month as well. They would both be celebrating on the same day!

She said to him, "I am like you in that, but I am the very reverse of you in other things."

Spurgeon replied, "Then you must be a good woman!"

She said, "No, that is not what I mean."

He said, "But are you not a believer?"

"Well," she answered, "I ... I try to be."

He took her by the hand, and said, "You are not telling me that you try to believe my Lord Jesus Christ? When your mother was about, did you say to her, 'Mother, I will try and believe you'? No, you would believe her because she was true, and you must believe Jesus Christ."

"Sir," she said, "do pray for me."

Maybe surprisingly, Spurgeon answered, "No, I am not inclined to do that! What should I pray for you about? If you will not believe my Lord, what blessing can He give you? What has He ever done that you should say, 'I cannot believe Him'?"

And again she said, " I will try!"

Spurgeon then quoted to her *John 3:36, "He who believes in the Son has everlasting life."*

She responded by saying, "I have been looking to my feelings, and this has been my mistake."

What matters is not trying but trusting. Don't try to trust—just trust!

45

An Unexpected Visit

"Blessed is that servant whom his master will find so doing when he comes."
Luke 12:43

Sometimes people make arrangements to visit you. They might say, "Can I come round on Saturday afternoon at 3 o'clock?" If that is convenient, you get ready for them. Perhaps you tidy your room, and maybe your mother puts the kettle on, ready to give them a drink when they arrive. But some people just call, without any prior warning. You are not expecting them, but there they are, knocking on your door!

Spurgeon, as you will know, was a very busy man, but, of course, sometimes he would go to visit people who were members of the Tabernacle. One day he called on one of the ladies of the church without telling her beforehand. He just came uninvited and unexpected!

What would your family have done if they had known Spurgeon was calling? Your mother would probably insist on hoovering the carpet, your father would get out the best crockery for tea, and you would be told to wash your face, put some clean clothes on and be on your best behaviour! But it would be more difficult if he called unexpectedly, wouldn't it?

When Spurgeon arrived at the lady's house, there she was on her knees, cleaning and whitening the front steps of her house! Can you imagine how she felt? As soon as she saw him coming, she got very flustered and embarrassed!

"Oh dear, sir," she said, "I did not know you were coming today, or I would have been ready!"

Knowing something about Spurgeon, how do you think he reacted?

Well, he pointed out to her that she was ready, for she was doing what she ought to be doing. He said, "When the Lord Jesus Christ comes suddenly, I hope He will find me doing as you were doing, namely, fulfilling the duty of the hour."

When later he retold the story, he said, "I thought she looked more beautiful with her pail beside her than if she had been dressed according to the latest fashion!"

The Lord Jesus Christ is going to come again to this world, not this time as a baby, but as the Lord and King of Glory. When will that be? No one knows. A much more important question is, what should we be doing when He comes? You might like to read the parable of the faithful servant and the evil servant which Jesus told in Luke's Gospel, chapter 12 verses 35–48. The faithful servant was doing his duty when his master returned—that is, just the ordinary things that he had been given to do. If we are alive when Jesus returns, the same should be true of us. Jesus said, *"Blessed is that servant whom his master will find so doing when he comes" (Luke 12:43)*.

46

Telling Others

"... tell them what great things the Lord has done for you ..."
Mark 5:19

A Christian always wants other people to become Christians, too. We want the Lord Who saved us to save others as well. The Lord Jesus said the gospel—the good news about forgiveness and eternal life through faith in Him—should be told to everybody in the world! The first Christians took that great commission very seriously, and you can read in the book of Acts how the news went further and further afield, and how many people came to trust in the Saviour. It has been like that for the last two thousand years. All the time, new people are hearing the message, and the Lord is constantly adding to His worldwide church.

I want you to think just now about how the gospel can be spread today.

People can find out about the way of salvation through:

- preaching and teaching
- Sunday schools
- Bible clubs
- tracts and books
- door-to-door visitation
- radio and television
- the Internet
- personal testimonies
- missions and crusades

Maybe you can think of some other ways.

One day a Christian man was talking to Spurgeon, and he asked him what he could do about winning others to Christ. Spurgeon asked him, "What are you? What do you do?" The man answered, "I am an engine driver."

Do you know what kind of trains were running then? They were steam trains. You can still see and even ride on them today in some places.

In the cab of the engine there would be the driver and another man called a fireman. He wasn't there to put out a fire. He was there to do the opposite—it was his job to shovel coal into the engine to keep the fire going, otherwise the train would stop!

Spurgeon asked the man, "Is your fireman a Christian?" He answered, "I don't know!" Spurgeon said, "Go back, and find out, and start on him!"

Some young Christians might dream of being a missionary or a great preacher, but what we all should do is to start where God has placed us, and it is there that He expects us to serve Him. Maybe, if you trust Him, He might call you to do something else later, but the important thing is to serve Him now—just where you are.

There was a demon-possessed man whom Jesus healed, and he wanted to go with Jesus, but he was told, *"Go home to your friends, and tell them what great things the Lord has done for you, and how He has had compassion on you" (Mark 5:19).*

47

Would You Exchange?

"For what will it profit a man if he gains the whole world, and loses his own soul?"
Mark 8:36

Spurgeon met lots of people, and all sorts—young and old, rich and poor, believers and unbelievers. One day he got into conversation with a young man who was very rich. He had everything that the world could offer! He said to Spurgeon, "I cannot stand Christian people! Their religion does not make them cheerful or happy, and they are always moaning and groaning and complaining."

Spurgeon said, "Come along with me, my friend, and we will visit one of your complaining Christians!"

He took the young man to a block of flats. They went inside, up a lot of stairs, right up to a room in the attic. There, in front of a fireplace, sat an elderly woman. Was she warming herself by the fire? No! There was no fire in the fireplace because she was so poor that she couldn't afford coal or wood. And she was doubled up with rheumatism and in a lot of pain.

Spurgeon asked her, "How is your rheumatism today?"

She answered, "Oh, it is so bad, and it never gets any better!"

Spurgeon then said to her, "Well, my friend, look at this young man. He is rich, he is healthy and strong, and he has every pleasure that earth can give him, and he is without God in the world. Tell me now, would you change with him?"

Well, what a change or swap that would be! Exchanging old age for youth! Exchanging illness for health! Exchanging poverty for riches! That sounds good, doesn't it? But on the other hand, it would mean exchanging trust for unbelief, exchanging spiritual life for spiritual death, exchanging the promise of heaven for the dread of hell. That doesn't really sound like a good bargain after all!

What do you think the old woman said? Well, all she could say was this: "Change with HIM?" By that she meant, "Not at any price!"

I'm sure that that lady knew the words of the Lord Jesus. He said, *"For what will it profit a man if he gains the whole world, and loses his own soul?" (Mark 8:36)*. There is a hymn that would have fitted well into her mouth:

> I'd rather than Jesus than silver or gold.
> I'd rather be His than have riches untold;
> I'd rather have Jesus than houses or lands;
> I'd rather be led by His nail-pierced hand!

48
War

"... all who take the sword will perish by the sword."
Matthew 26:52

It is very sad that almost all the time there are wars being fought somewhere in the world. In the twentieth century there were two world wars—do you know the years during which they were fought? Millions of people were killed in those conflicts—soldiers in the various armies, as well as many civilians, men, women and children. Cities and towns, far away from the front lines, were bombed. See if you can find out if the town where you live was bombed. Do you know of any more recent wars? Not many years ago, our country was involved in the Falklands War and later on, in the Gulf War. In all the fighting, of course, many people are killed and injured.

When Spurgeon was the pastor of the Tabernacle in London, a war was being fought between France and Germany. He produced his own magazine called *The Sword and Trowel*, and in it he wrote a letter to the two leaders of those countries—to Napoleon, the Emperor of France and to William, the King of Prussia.

He wrote, "If you must fight, why don't you strip and go at it yourselves? It is cowardly of you to send a lot of other fellows to be shot on your account. I don't like fighting at all, but really, if it would save the lives of millions, I would not mind taking care of your jackets while you had a set-to with fisticuffs! … Did either of you ever think what war means? Why, if you are made of flesh and blood, the sight of one poor wounded man, with the blood oozing out of him, will make you feel sick!"

Then he went on to say that he didn't like to see any animal in pain, but how much worse it is to see men in pain! He wrote, "Stop this war, if you can, at once, and turn to some better business than killing men!"

I don't know if Napoleon or William ever saw Spurgeon's open letter to them, but if they did, surely it must have made them think!

Today, sadly, fighting and war are often glorified. Many films and games make war sound exciting, and boys especially like fighting! Cowboys and Indians, soldiers firing guns, wars in space! We need to remember that real war is a terrible thing. It brings suffering, sadness and loss.

When men came to arrest Jesus in the Garden of Gethsemane, Peter got a sword and cut off the ear of a servant of the high priest. He loved Jesus and wanted to protect Him, and save Him from His enemies. But Jesus said, *"Put your sword in its place, for all who take the sword will perish by the sword" (Matthew 26:52).*

49

Is It Real?

"Today, if you hear His voice, do not harden your hearts."
Hebrews 3:15

One house in which Spurgeon lived in London was quite close to Wimbledon Common, and, of course, the Common is still there today. You might have been there yourself. Maybe you have heard of the Wombles, make-believe furry creatures who supposedly lived in burrows on the Common and who collected and recycled rubbish! Books were written about them and a television series for children was broadcast some years ago.

One day Spurgeon was sitting with a friend in his living room and the windows were open because it was a nice, warm day. And then, quite suddenly, they heard, "Bang! Bang! Boom! Boom!" Guns and cannons were being fired on the Common! If you had been there, it might well have given you a fright.

Yet Spurgeon and his friend were not worried at all, and I'll tell you why. They had already been told that military manoeuvres were going to take place on the Common. Soldiers were going to try out their rifles and cannons, and so all the noise of the cracks of the rifles and the thunder of the cannons was nothing to be alarmed about. There was no real fighting and there was no danger!

Spurgeon's friend said, "Supposing there were really a war there, we should not sit quite so comfortably in our room with the windows open listening to all this noise!" Because they knew it was just a practice they didn't worry. They knew that it wasn't a real battle.

What happened that day and the comment of his friend, made Spurgeon think of the fact that many people hear about the Lord Jesus Christ, they hear about God, they hear about heaven and hell, but they think, "It's not real so it's got nothing to do with me."

We all need to know what is real and what is not. I mentioned the Wombles, but they are not real animals. There might be nice, funny, interesting stories about them, and maybe some boys and girls have been encouraged not to drop litter, and to put rubbish in bins, and even help to recycle things which are no longer wanted. But Wombles are just make-believe creatures in story books.

The Lord Jesus Christ came into human history 2,000 years ago. He really lived and died on the cross, and He really rose from the dead. He is today just as alive as you are, and He is in heaven now. God is real. Heaven and hell are real.

Make-believe stories may be interesting, but the stories of the Bible are true. That is why we are told, *"Today, if you hear His voice, do not harden your hearts ..." (Hebrews 3:15).*

50

A Diary

"For to me, to live is Christ."
Philippians 1:21

Do you have a diary? Most people do. I know that I would get into an awful muddle if I didn't have one and keep it up-to-date. I'll let you into a secret—I have two diaries, one for what I plan to do and one for what I have already done. One for the future and one for the past! In fact, I started keeping a diary when I was nine years old, and I've kept all the 'past' ones, which means I've got a huge number of them!

Spurgeon kept a diary, too—at least he did when he was a young man. In it he described how he was converted. Maybe you remember the story: how, when he was fifteen years old, one very snowy Sunday morning he went into a little chapel in Colchester, and there God worked in his heart. He turned from his sins and trusted in the Lord Jesus Christ. He also recorded how he witnessed for Jesus in those early years, and about his first pastorate in Waterbeach in Cambridgeshire. After he had moved to London he met and fell in love with Susannah, and they got married. Soon afterwards he gave his diary to her, but asked that it should not be read until after his death. She agreed. Maybe she was tempted, but she kept her promise and didn't read it until four years after he had died.

I wonder what happened to that diary! No one knows. Maybe it was somehow destroyed, but there are many people who would like to read it. I know I would! Perhaps I might have found some other stories in it to write down for you!

However, I can tell you something from it. He hadn't been a Christian for very long when he wrote these words, "I vow to glory alone in Jesus, and His cross, and to spend my life in the extension of His cause, in whatsoever way He pleases. I desire to be sincere in this solemn profession, having but one object in view, and that to glorify God. Help me to honour Thee, and live the life of Christ on earth."

Sadly, many people have no aim in life. They don't know why they are here, living on planet earth. They have no real reason for living. As they get older, and maybe face death, they might ask, "What's it all been about? Is that all there is to life?"

We all ought to ask ourselves, "What am I living for? Who am I living for?" Spurgeon had his answer to those questions, and he would have put it in one word: Christ! The apostle Paul felt the same. He wrote, *"For to me, to live is Christ" (Philippians 1:21)*. The best and greatest thing is to live for the Lord Jesus Christ, for His honour and glory.

51

You Can See Better on a Sunday

"Call the Sabbath a delight ..."
Isaiah 58:13

One of Spurgeon's friends was going to move up to Newcastle-upon-Tyne, in the northeast of England. It might be helpful if you got out a map and looked for that city, and when you have found it, keep your finger there. The landlord of a newly built house that was for rent was showing him round. Maybe you and your family have moved house. Even if you haven't, imagine looking round a place into which you might move. You would look everywhere, wouldn't you? You would go into all the rooms downstairs, and those upstairs, and you would wonder which might be your bedroom! You would inspect the house very carefully!

That, of course, is what Spurgeon's friend did. He looked round downstairs, and then went upstairs. He went into one of the rooms and looked out of the window. Then the landlord said something very strange. He said, "You can see Durham Cathedral from here on a Sunday!"

Have another look at the map. Can you see Durham? It is about twenty miles south of Newcastle.

Spurgeon's friend couldn't understand what the landlord meant. He asked, "Why on a Sunday more than any other day?" How could you see on a Sunday what you could not see on any other day of the week?

Before you read any further, can you guess the reason?

Here is a clue: Newcastle then was a great industrial city, with many factories with their big chimneys.

The landlord's answer was this, "Well, the furnaces are not going, and the smoke is not rising to darken the atmosphere on a Sunday!"

On Mondays right through to Saturdays the factories were working, and black smoke was belching out from the chimneys, and nobody could see very far. But on Sundays they were closed, and there was little smoke to obscure the view.

Spurgeon drew out a lesson from his friend's experience. Sometimes life during the week is very "smoky"—in other words, there are so many things to think about—your studies, your friends, your responsibilities. Although we ought to have a quiet time with the Lord every day, reading the Bible and praying, we have many other things to think about, too. But on Sundays most of the 'smoke' of our daily lives is not there, and so we can spend longer thinking about spiritual things and we can see them more clearly. Having Sunday as a different day is a privilege as well as a duty! *"If you turn away your foot from the Sabbath, from doing your pleasure on My holy day, and call the Sabbath a delight, the holy day of the LORD honorable, and shall honor Him, not doing your own ways, nor finding your own pleasure, nor speaking your own words, then you shall delight yourself in the LORD" (Isaiah 58:13–14).*

52
Backsliding

They "went backward and not forward."
Jeremiah 7:24

All the stories that I have told you about Spurgeon have been true ones: they really happened. But for the last story in this book I want to tell you one that is not true, although many people believed that it was!

When Spurgeon was the pastor at the New Park Street church (before the Metropolitan Tabernacle was built) he was preaching one Sunday about how Christians can backslide—that is how easy it is to stop going forward in the Christian life. And if we stop going forward, then we start going backwards! We can't stay still. Going backwards means that we slip into old sinful habits, and we don't enjoy the Lord and His presence. Spurgeon wanted to make that point very clear. See if you can guess what he was supposed to have done next. Think of a pulpit with steps going up to it, and imagine Spurgeon in the pulpit. He wanted to make the point that going down is easy, and going up is difficult. So what did he do? If you live in a house with stairs up to your bedroom, maybe you have done this, although I don't advise you to do it because it can be dangerous! Any ideas?

The story goes that Spurgeon got on the banisters or hand rail of the pulpit steps and slid down! What a sight that would have been, especially because he was a little portly and not exactly thin! And then, having slid all the way down, he struggled to pull himself up the banisters and get back into the pulpit again!

This story was told by many people, and some even said that they had actually seen him do it! One pastor in America publicly said that he had been in the church that day, and had witnessed it.

Spurgeon heard the story, and he said that it was not true. He also pointed out that at that time the pulpit was fixed in the church wall and entered from the vestry behind, and so there was no way that he could have slid down any banister in the church, because there wasn't one there!

But the story makes a point! How easy to slide down, to backslide spiritually, to be out of near contact with the Lord Jesus. And how difficult to get back to where we were before. The Lord complained of His people in Old Testament times in this way: *"Yet they did not obey or incline their ear, but followed the counsels and the dictates of their evil hearts, and went backward and not forward" (Jeremiah 7:24)*. Because the Lord is so kind and gracious, He is always ready and willing to welcome us back, like the father in the parable of the prodigal son. But if you are a child of God, your motto should be, "Forward ... with the Lord!"

About Day One:

Day One's threefold commitment:

- To be faithful to the Bible, God's inerrant, infallible Word
- To be relevant to our modern generation
- To be excellent in our publication standards

I continue to be thankful for the publications of Day One. They are biblical; they have sound theology; and they are relevant to the issues at hand. The material is condensed and manageable while, at the same time, being complete—a challenging balance to find. We are happy in our ministry to make use of these excellent publications.

JOHN MACARTHUR, PASTOR-TEACHER, GRACE COMMUNITY CHURCH, CALIFORNIA

It is a great encouragement to see Day One making such excellent progress. Their publications are always biblical, accessible and attractively produced, with no compromise on quality. Long may their progress continue and increase!

JOHN BLANCHARD, AUTHOR, EVANGELIST AND APOLOGIST

The answer to the question in Story 3, 'A Sad Story', is 4,000 miles.